AF512751

NYĀYA-VAIŚEṢIKA PHILOSOPHY

AND

TEXT SCIENCE

NYĀYA-VAIŚEṢIKA PHILOSOPHY AND TEXT SCIENCE

Katsunori Hirano

MOTILAL BANARSIDASS PUBLISHERS
PRIVATE LIMITED • DELHI

First Edition: Delhi, 2012

© Katsunori Hirano
All Rights Reserved

ISBN: 978-81-208-3558-0

MOTILAL BANARSIDASS
41 U.A. Bungalow Road, Jawahar Nagar, Delhi 110 007
8 Mahalaxmi Chamber, 22 Bhulabhai Desai Road, Mumbai 400 026
203 Royapettah High Road, Mylapore, Chennai 600 004
236, 9th Main III Block, Jayanagar, Bengaluru 560 011
Sanas Plaza, 1302 Baji Rao Road, Pune 411 002
8 Camac Street, Kolkata 700 017
Ashok Rajpath, Patna 800 004
Chowk, Varanasi 221 001

Printed in India

By RP Jain at NAB Printing Unit,
A-44, Naraina, Phase-I, New Delhi 110 028
and Published by JP Jain for
Motilal Banarsidass Publishers (P) Ltd, 40-41 U.A.
Bungalow Road, Jawahar Nagar, Delhi 110 007

ACKNOWLEDGMENTS

Under the 21st Century COE (Centers of Excellence) Program, which was carried out by the Ministry of Education, Culture, Sports, Science and Technology of Japan, a part of the staff of the School of Letters, Nagoya University, promoted the project titled "Studies for the Integrated Text Science," in order to clarify the meaning-system of texts. The project used the term "text" to refer to an implement of communication—for instance, language, figures, bodily action, and so forth—and then inquired, in numerous ways, into the question of what system, for generating meaning, each text has. Through this project we hoped to formulate a universal theory—named, in our work, Universal Grammar—capable of explaining, beyond the different forms of these texts, "the system of the generation of meaning" common to each. As a member of this project, I have devoted myself to the study of the meaning-system of the commentary text in classical Indian philosophy. In turn, it was mainly through discussions with the members of the COE program that I was inspired to write the present book.

I wish to express my deepest gratitude to Professor Shoichi Sato, the head of the COE program, a member of the Japan Academy, and the retired head of the Department of Occidental History, Graduate School of Letters, Nagoya University, who gave me excellent working conditions and an intellectual environment for concentrating on my research. I shall never forget his help and encouragement. I also wish to extend my deepest gratitude to Professor Toshihiro Wada, head of the Department of Indian Studies, Graduate School of Letters, Nagoya University, for his constant help and encouragement. Many years ago, it was he who initiated me into Sanskrit and Nyāya-Vaiśeṣika studies. Without his generous help, this book would never have been completed.

Throughout my studies, I have received kind assistance from many individuals. I am grateful to Professor Junsho Kato, the retired head of the Department of Indian Studies, Graduate School of Letters, Nagoya University, who also initiated me in Sanskrit and Buddhist studies. Professor Akira Suganuma, Professor Emeritus of Toyo University, initiated me into Indian study. Professor Yoshiaki Koike, Professor Emeritus of Toyo University, taught me to have an interest of science.

Fortunately I was able to study at the University of Pune under the Nagoya-Pune Exchange Program from September 1998 to August 1999, being provided scholarship from the Ministry of Education, Culture, Sports, Science and Technology of Japan. And I would like to express my deepest gratitude to Professor V.N. Jha, the retired head of the Centre of Advanced Study in Sanskrit, University of Pune, whose clear explanation enabled me to understand Prācīna Vaiśeṣika philosophy. I wish to thank Professor Ujjwara Jha, the head of the Centre of Advanced Study in Sanskrit, University of Pune, who gave me invaluable suggestions for understanding Nyāya philosophy. I also wish to extend my deepest gratitude to Professor Saroja Bhate, the retired head of the Department of Sanskrit, University of Pune, who admitted me to study at this University. I also wish to thank Dr. Yashodara Kar, University of Pune, who gave me invaluable suggestions for understanding the Vyākarana.

In December 2005, as a part of the COE project, we held the seventh international conference under the title, "Conflict between Tradition and Creativity in Indian Philosophy: Text and Context." I would like to express my sincere gratitude to all of the guest speakers: Professor Johannes Bronkhorst, Faculté des Letters, Université de Lausanne, Professor Masahiro Shimoda, Graduate School of Humanities and Sociology, University of Tokyo, and Professor Parimal G. Patil, John L. Loeb Associate Professor of the Humanities, Committee on the Study of Religious and Department of Sanskrit and Indian Studies, Harvard University (See Bronkhorst [2010], Shimoda [2010], and Patil [2010]). They gave me invaluable comments and suggestions. I also wish to thank the audience of the conference who gave me invaluable comments which helped in the formulation of this book.

This book contains several of my previously published papers, which have been reproduced with some modification. I am grateful to the Graduate School of Letters, Nagoya University, for permission to incorporate Hirano [2003] [2004c] [2005] [2006b] [2009] [2010b]; to Professor T. Wada for his permission to incorporate Hirano [2010a] and to Professor Kuruvilla Pandikattu SJ for his permission to incorporate Hirano [forthcoming] into this book.

I am also deeply indebted to Dr. Matthew Pelowski, Nagoya University, who carefully read over the manuscript of the present book and corrected my English.

Finally, I would like to thank my deceased father, Harumi Hirano, and my mother, Fusae Hirano, without whose generous support and encouragement I could not have continued my study. I also wish to thank my wife, Misa and my child, Gaku. Without her warm heart and his lovely smiles, this book would not have been completed.

K. HIRANO
Nagoya
September 2011

CONTENTS

PART I

THE MEANING-SYSTEM

OF

THE COMMENTARY TEXT

INTRODUCTION

The present book aims to clarify what system for generating meaning the commentary text in classical Indian philosophy has. This question has not been sufficiently addressed and answered from the philological viewpoint. In turn, in this book, I have attempted an answer from an alternative perspective, utilizing the approach of "text science." However, this does not mean that such an attempt can be accomplished independently of the previous accomplishments through the philological method. The dependence of this book on these accomplishments can be immediately realized with a glance at the Bibliography. And it is this foundation of scholarship that has enabled this book to, hopefully, go further, analyzing the Indian philosophic commentary text from the viewpoint of text science and to, again hopefully, show a new aspect of Indian philosophy. Text science attempts to establish a universal theory functioning throughout all human expression, including behavior. Human expression, in other words, the implement of communication, has various forms—language, figures, bodily action, etc., etc. Text science considers all of these means of communication to be "texts" and attempts to establish the meaning-system of the text as a universal theory beyond the different forms of texts themselves. We might state the character of text science as follows:

> *Setting the form of a text above its contents,*[1] *text science attempts to clarify a meaning-system which is inherent in each text and to show the common meaning-system among the texts. However, the inquiry of the form is not irrelevant to the inquiry of the contents. Although each inquiry seems to be different on the surface, both are relative in their depths; the form influences the contents as*

1. McLuhan [1964] was an early proponent for paying attention to the nature of media itself, rather than its contents.

long as the contents are conveyed through the form. Therefore, text science is not a viewpoint which ignores the contents of texts.

Following this approach, my book has clarified the particular meaning-system of the commentary text in classical Indian philosophy. Therefore, by showing this system for generating meaning in the commentary text, we might elicit new understanding of the contents of a preceding text, which is disclosed from analyzing its form. This book sets out to uncover this mechanism.

This book also includes an annotated translation of the "chapter on the definition of inherence" (*samavāya*) in the commentary texts on the *Padārthadharmasaṃgraha* (*PDhS*) of Praśastapāda (ca. 550–600)[2] of the Vaiśeṣika school. The commentary texts are the *Vyomavatī* (*Vy*) of Vyomaśiva (ca. 900–960), the *Nyāyakandalī* (*NK*) of Śrīdhara (ca. 950–1000), and the *Kiraṇāvalī* (*Kir*) of Udayana (ca. 1050–1100). These commentary texts, in particular their chapters of inherence, are important for investigating not only Vaiśeṣika philosophy, but also the controversy between the Vaiśeṣika and Buddhist philosophers, since the concept of inherence played an essential role in the Vaiśeṣika doctrine and, therefore, was a target for criticism from the opponents. It is through dealing with the chapter of inherence's definition in these three commentaries texts that this book has considered the meaning-system of the commentary text. Therefore, my book is useful for those who are interested in the thoughts of the Nyāya-Vaiśeṣika school and the Buddhist Logic school, as well as for those who are interested in a new interpretation of Indian philosophy.

My research, since 2003 under the COE program, has focused mainly on this definition of inherence as commented on in the *Vy*, the *NK*, and the *Kir*. While the present book is based mainly on my previous articles, published after 2003, many of which are reproduced partially or in full here, it should be noted that this book is not merely a collection or reproduction of these papers. This book consists of four parts: Part I considers the commentary text from a viewpoint of text science; and Parts II, III, and IV present each annotated translation of the "definition of inherence" chapter in the commentary texts on the

2. On the dates of authors referred to in this book, see Potter (ed.) [1995a (1970)] [1995b (1977): 9–12]. When I have followed other sources on their dates, I have referred to the sources in the footnotes.

PDhS; the *Vy*, the *NK*, and the *Kir*. Part I is further divided into five chapters.

Chapter 1, "Background History and Methodology," presents a background meant to aid in understanding the following chapters. For this task this chapter briefly explains the history and doctrine of the Vaiśeṣika school, the commentary texts on the *PDhS*, the concept of "inherence relation," and the concept of "text science."

Chapter 2, "Analysis of the Commentary Text from the Communication Theory," clarifies a particular system of the commentary text, which is explained from a viewpoint of communication theory. Furthermore this chapter shows the effectiveness of the commentary text in conveying knowledge, in a particular context which regards the criticism of authoritative thought as a religious sin, by propounding the question of why the commentary text was chosen as a main implement of communication for conveying knowledge in classical Indian philosophy. This chapter is based on Hirano [2003] [2004a].

Chapter 3, "Originality and Quotation," clarifies an aspect of the system of the commentary text, considering the genesis of commentary texts from a viewpoint of quotation theory, and utilizing the "chapter of inherence's definition" in the *Vy*, the *NK*, and the *Kir*. I first consider the concept of "definition" as the act of *defining* the meaning of a defined object through the exclusion of other objects. Then I analyze this process in the three commentary texts, discussing what each commentary text "excludes" via four factors composing inherence's definition in the *PDhD*. That is to say, I analyze the combination between each factor and what is excluded in each commentary text. As a result, I reach the conclusion that a commentary text is generated through the explicit or implicit "quotation" from the precedent text, and the originality of thought in the following text is accomplished by these new combinations between the factor and what is excluded. This chapter represents, for the most part, a revision of Hirano [2004c] [2010a].

Chapter 4, "Interaction between Text and Context," clarifies a system of the commentary text, analyzing the genesis of the commentary text while taking context into consideration. In this chapter, I have analyzed the main point of the arguments in each of the *Vy*, the *NK*, and the *Kir* by measuring the proportion of comments on the four factors (parts) composing inherence's definition in the *PDhS*. As a possible cause for the difference and the change in point of emphasis between the three commentary texts, I anticipate the existence of objections from opponents, which function as a context for commentary. I then conclude that the commentary text is generated under the influence of this context. This chapter represents a revision of Hirano [2005].

Chapter 5, "Conclusion," shows the meaning-system of the commentary text based on the arguments in Chapters 2, 3, and 4. I explore this meaning-system of the commentary text in classical Indian philosophy, considering this particular process whereby interpretation of the original text and answers to counterarguments interact with one another in the form of quotation under the influence of their context. Further, the system of the commentary text is marked by an open nature. This chapter represents a revision of Hirano [2006b].

Part II, Part III, and Part IV, which provide philological material for the present study, contain my translation of the "chapter of inherence's definition" in each commentary text on the *PDhS*—the *Vy*, the *NK*, and the *Kir*. Part II, "An Annotated Translation of the Definition of Inherence (*samavāya*) Chapter in the *Vyomavatī*," is based on Hirano [forthcoming]. Part III, "An Annotated Translation of the Definition of Inherence (*samavāya*) Chapter in the *Nyāyakandalī*," is based on Hirano [2009]. Part IV, "An Annotated Translation of the Definition of Inherence (*samavāya*) Chapter in the *Kiraṇāvalī*," is based on Hirano [2010b]. When translating the *NK* and the *Kir*, I have consulted three commentary texts on the *NK* and on the *Kir* respectively. These commentaries were of great help in reading the more difficult portions of the *NK* and the *Kir*. However, when we look to current scholarship, no one has yet completely translated this chapter in the *Vy* and the *Kir* into English. In turn, although a complete translation of this portion in the *NK* is available, my translation provides a detailed explanation of the concepts and terms mentioned, consulting the other chapters in the *NK* and the commentary texts. Moreover, a synopsis of this work is presented with my translation.

It must be noted here that there is a possibility that the presented answer for the key question of this book is based upon an exceptional case, since this book deals with the "inherence's definition chapters" in three commentary texts of the Vaiśeṣika only. However, these materials, though specific, are also commentary texts. And therefore we might say that the presented answer in this book has relevance to that of the general discussion of commentary texts in Indian philosophy. In turn, if we cannot at least explain the meaning-system of these small materials, we cannot hope to construct an explanation for that of commentary texts in general.

Lastly, one major innovation of my book is to show various aspects of the commentary text in Indian philosophy by applying concepts used in text science; for instance, communication theory, quotation theory, and contextualism. It is through the new application of this method of analysis, I firmly believe, that we will be lead to new understanding of Indian philosophy, which cannot be achieved by only reading philosophical texts of classical India and which might make an important contribution to the field of Indian study itself.

Chapter 1

Background History and Methodology

1.1 History of the Vaiśeṣika School

The Vaiśeṣika, the philosophical school responsible for the texts that this book will analyze, is counted among the so-called six orthodox systems of Hindu thought in ancient India, accompanied also by the Vedānta, Mīmāṃsā, Sāṃkhya, Yoga, and Nyāya.[1] The Vaiśeṣika is said to have been founded by the mythical figure Kaṇāda. Although the date of Kaṇāda's existence is not ascertained, it seems that he flourished around the 2nd century B.C.[2]

We can set the beginning of the history of Vaiśeṣika philosophy at the writing of the *Vaiśeṣikasūtra* (*VS*), which is the only work attributed to Kaṇāda. The thought put down in the *VS* then became the basis text for the succeeding scholars of the school. This was followed by the commentary text, *Padārthadharmasaṃgraha* (*PDhS*) or *Praśastapādabhāṣya*, by Praśastapāda (ca. 550–600). The *PDhS* reconstructed Vaiśeṣika's teaching and became an authoritative text itself, together with the earlier *VS*. Following this, numerous commentary texts were then provided to the *PDhS* as follows:[3]

(1) The *Vyomavatī* of Vyomaśiva (ca. 900–960),
(2) The *Nyāyakandalī* of Śrīdhara (ca. 950–1000),

---

1. Regarding the historical development of the concept of "six systems of Indian philosophy," see Marui [2002].
2. Kaṇāda had a number of other names: Kaṇabhakṣa, Kaṇabhuji, Kaṇāśin, Kaṇavrata, Kaṇacara (rice-grain-eater), Ulūka (owl), and Kāśyapa (descent of the sage Kaśyapa). Regarding the date and other names of Kaṇāda, see Potter (ed.) [1995b (1977): 211–212] and Thakur [2003: 3–6].
3. On the commentary texts on the *PDhS*, see Matilal [1977: 67–68].

(3) The *Kiraṇāvalī* of Udayana (ca. 1050–1100),
(4) The *Līlāvatī* of Śrīvatsa (ca. 1000–1050),
(5) The *Kaṇādarahasya* of Śaṅkaramiśra (ca. 1430),
(6) The *Bhāṣyanikarṣa* of Mallinātha (ca. 1450),
(7) The *Setu* of Padmanābhamiśra (ca. 1560), and
(8) The *Śūkti* of Jagadīṣa (ca. 1620).

Among these eight commentary texts on the *PDhS*, number 4, the *Līlāvatī* of Śrīvatsa, is yet to be discovered.

The Vaiśeṣika school subsequently developed into the Navya-nyāya school (New Nyāya school) with the Prācīna Nyāya school (Old Nyāya school). Regarding this origin of the Navya-nyāya school, there are two views. One is that the school began from Udayana, who is the author of (3) the *Kiraṇāvalī*. The other theory is that the founding can be attributed to Gaṅgeśa (ca. 1320).[4]

1.2 The Vaiśeṣika Categories

The Vaiśeṣika philosophical system is marked by categorization, dividing the outer world into six categories (*padārtha*)[5], and claiming that all entities can be listed and classified under a certain category. According to the *PDhS*, the six categories are listed as: substance (*dravya*), quality (*guṇa*), activity (*karman*), universal (*sāmānya*), particular (*viśeṣa*), and inherence (*samavāya*).[6] In the time of Udayana, a seventh category, absence (*abhāva*), was added to the original six categories.[7] These categories are then further subdivided into nine kinds of substances, twenty-four kinds of qualities, five kinds of activities and two kinds of universals. The number of particulars is endless, while there is only one inherence.[8] Table I summarizes the kinds of categories.

---

4. On the origin of Navya-nyāya, see Wada [2007: 9–23].
5. On the concept and the translation of *padārtha*, see Halbfass [1993 (1992): 76–78].
6. *PDhS*, no. 2: *dravyaguṇakarmasāmānyaviśeṣasamavāyānāṃ ṣaṇṇāṃ padārthānāṃ* ...
7. See the *Lakṣaṇāvalī*, p. 56, nos. 1–3 and Wada [2007: 6, n. 8].
8. On the explanation and the translations of Sanskrit words on categories, see Raju [1985: 253–262].

Table I: The Kinds of Categories in Vaiśeṣika Philosophy

Category	Kinds
Substance	earth, water, fire, air, ether, time, space, soul, mind
Quality	color, taste, smell, touch, number, magnitude, distinctness, conjunction, disjunction, nearness, remoteness, cognition, pleasure, pain, desire, hate, effort, weight, fluidity, viscidity, tendency, unseen merit, unseen demerit, sound
Activity	throwing upwards, throwing downwards, contraction, expansion, locomotion
Universal	being-ness (highest universal), cow-ness etc. (lower universal)
Particular	[endless]
Inherence	[one]

The Vaiśeṣika analyzes the world and explains its structure by these categories and their subdivisions.

1.3 The Concept of Inherence

The sixth category, inherence (*samavāya*), the focus of the study in this book, is the eternal relation—where the word "eternal" means that there is no cause in the existence of inherence. There is only one such inherence in the world. This eternal relation is established between entities that fix without being separate from each other (*ayutasiddha*).[9] The *PDhS* defines inherence as follows:

> *That which is the relation, being a cause of the idea "[this is] here (this is in that)," between entities that fix without being separate [from each other], which [stand as] the superstratum and the*

9. Jhā [1982 (1915): 35, n. 3] explains the word "*ayutasiddha*" as follows: The word "*Ayutasiddha*" means that which is *known* (*siddha*) as *not separate* (*a-yuta*)—the word "*yuta*" being derived from the root "*yu*" to separate. Regarding the English equivalent for "*ayutasiddha*," Jhā [1982 (1915): 32] and Ui [1917: 176, fn. 3] set "things that are inseparable," D.N. Shastri [1976 (1964): 380], Potter (ed.) [1995 (1997): 283], and Bhattacharya [1994: 18] "inseparable," Kannu [1992: 201] "inseparable things," Halbfass [1993 (1992): 147] "relata that are ... incapable of existing separately," and B. Shastri [1993: 116] "inseparably connected."

substratum, is inherence.[10]

(*PDhS*, no. 9: *ayutasiddhānām ādhāryādhārabhūtānāṃ yaḥ sambandha ihapratyayahetuḥ sa samavāyaḥ*.)

Inherence is between entities—for instance, between substance and quality, substance and activity, between a type of universal and a thing (*artha*: substance, quality, and activity), and between the whole (*avayavin*) and its parts (*avayavas*).[11] Examples of substance and quality are a pot and its color, fire and its hotness, and so on, where, for example, the pot's color, let us say blue, exists in the pot itself. Blue color cannot exist independently of the pot, and therefore the pot and its color are regarded as entities that fix without being separate from each other, that is to say, as inseparable entities. And the relation between these entities, according to the Vaiśeṣika, is inherence.[12]

We can illustrate this structure of the relation between the pot and its color in Figure 1.

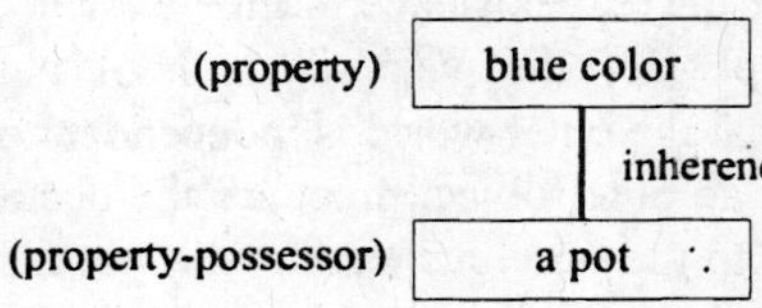

Figure 1

10. On the translation of inherence's definition in the *PDhS*, Jhā [1982 (1915): 32] translates it as: "Inherence is the relationship subsisting among things that are inseparable, standing to one another in the character of the container and the contained—such relationship being the basis of the idea that 'this is in that.'" Hirano [2009: 46] translates the inherence's definition in the *PDhS* into "The relation, which is a cause of the idea '[this is] here (this is in that),' between entities that are incapable of existing separately [and] that stand as the superstratum and the substratum, is inherence." In this book, the translation has been modified based on the understanding that the word, "*ādhāryādhārabhūtānāṃ*," modifies the word, "*ayutasiddhānām*." On the role of "*-bhūta*" as making attributive substantive in the compound, see Whitney [1997 (1924): 493] and Tubb and Boose [2007: 167–168]. Regarding Japanese translation of the *PDhS*, see Kanakura [1971], Nakamura [1979], and Miyamoto [2008].
11. On the cases where inherence is accepted, see the *PDhS* [no. 373–374].
12. On the studies of inherence in Nyāya-Vaiśeṣika philosophy, see Faddegon [1969 (1918): 126], Hiriyanna [1957: 107–120], D.N. Shastri [1976 (1964): 374–394], Sen [1985], Potter [1991: 117–144], B. Shastri [1993], and Bhattacharya [1994].

I will briefly explain how to read Figure 1. The rectangle labeled "blue color" represents property (*dharma*), and the rectangle labeled "a pot" represents its possessor (*dharmin*). The line between "blue color" and "a pot" represents a relation between the property and the possessor, where the property is designated as the superstratum, or the contained entity (*ādhārya*), and its possessor as the substratum, or the container entity (*ādhāra*).[13] In this case, the relation indicated by the thick line is inherence.

The concept of inherence forms one of the most debated topics of Indian philosophy. The points of the debate include whether or not the relation of inherence is the object of perception, and by what relation it resides in its relatum; and, subsequently, the problem of the whole and its parts is debated with reference to inherence.[14] Among these topics, the most fundamental is whether inherence has a *real* existence or not. The Vaiśeṣika school, which stands in the realism camp in general, insists on the real existence of inherence. On the other hand, the Buddhist, the Jaina, the Mīmāṃsaka, the Sāṃkhya and the Vedāntin do not accept this concept or the real existence of inherence.[15]

The entire philosophy of the Vaiśeṣika school is marked by realism. Realism holds that the outer world is independent of cognition, and that the existence of an outer object precedes the occurrence of its cognition.[16] If we return to the previous example, a pot, its blue color, and the resulting inherence, according to this worldview, are *a priori* real. They are independent of the cognition that a "blue color is in the pot," and the existence of these entities precedes the occurrence of their cognition and justifies the validness of this cognition. According to the Vaiśeṣika, valid cognition (*pramā*) always has counterparts in the outer world, and these counterparts are the six categories.

On the other hand, idealism, the opposite view to realism, holds that the outer world is dependent on cognition, and that the existence of an outer object is a construction of the mind (*kalpanā*). In idealism, at

13. On this explanation of Figure, I have followed Tachikawa [1981: 18] and Wada [1990: 47–48] [2007: 29–30].
14. The concept of the whole (*avayavin*) plays a significant role in the debate about the existence of God between the Naiyāyika and the Buddhist, see Vattanky [1984: 40–41].
15. See B. Shastri [1993: 205–234].
16. On the concept of "realism," see Tachikawa [1981: 9–10], Umesha [1987: 22–26], Phillips [1997 (1996): 1], Murakami [1997: 33–35], and Hirano [2004b].

the moment of the cognition that a "blue color is in the pot," the cause of the cognition is not the existence of an outer object, but the mind itself.[17]

1.4 The Concept of Text

Having briefly introduced the historical and philosophical basis for this book, let us move on to the procedural basis for the following discussion—the concept of a text.

We have various implements for conveying our thoughts or expressing a certain feeling to others—words, music, painting, dancing, etc. Each of these implements can be further subdivided; for instance, the subdivisions of words might be chat, debate, poems, novels, treatises, newspapers, etc., and those of painting could be counted as abstract paintings, realism, etc. When we communicate with others, we carefully select one of these implements in order to convey, to others, certain information effectively. The word "effectively" here does not imply the absolute superiority or inferiority of particular implements, but the achieved degree of the senders' intentions or purposes concerning what and how they want to inform others (the receivers). The degree of this achievement depends on the suitability of the implement to the situation.

For instance, in the situation where one wants to quickly inform others of a great house fire, no one would choose the means of painting a fire on paper, without very special intentions or conditions. Most people would instead select words from among possible implements and shout "fire" to others, since words are more suitable for informing others of an occurrence more quickly than painting in this situation. In another example, however, where one wants to inform others of a certain thin shade of blue, painting might be more suitable for informing others.

This then raises the question, what causes some implement to be more suitable to convey thoughts to others in a particular situation? As a possible cause, we could expect that each implement has a particular meaning-system, which itself generates meaning, and which enables

17. B. Shastri [1993] and Bhattacharya [1994] show the points of debate about inherence between the Nyāya-Vaiśeṣika school and the Buddhist, the Jaina, and so on.

an implement to convey information to others more effectively in a particular situation and context. In turn, we could assume that, in the above examples, words have a meaning-system, which enables one to convey thoughts to others more quickly in the case of a large fire.

In this book I will use the term "text" to refer to these implements of communication, which themselves have a particular meaning-system. According to this usage, we can consider the above commentary "works" in classical Indian philosophy to be "texts" as well. It is from this viewpoint that this book will proceed, analyzing the meaning-system of the commentary text in classical Indian philosophy, centered around the Vaiśeṣika discussion of Inherence, from the theories of communication, quotation, and context.

Chapter 2

Analysis of the Commentary Text from the Communication Theory

2.1 Introduction

In Chapter 2, we consider the commentary text in Indian philosophy from the viewpoint of communication theory, in order to show the particular system of this commentary text and its effectiveness in informing knowledge in a particular context, and to advance an explanation for why, within our chosen context, it was mainly used as an implement of communication, from among several genres of texts, in order to impart knowledge to persons.

We will begin by examining how knowledge was transmitted from generation to generation in classical India. Specifically, the educational system will be examined from its organizational and individual aspects. The aim of examining this is to understand the particular context in which a commentary text was generated.[1] Next, through explaining the basic concepts of the elements in communication theory, this theory will be applied to the commentary text itself. Consequently, it will be clear that the commentary text is composed of two kinds of communication in which, in each case, the commentator is considered to be the receiver. Then, from the interaction between these two forms of communication, we will consider the effectiveness of the particular system of the commentary text for imparting knowledge and will give an assertion as to why the commentary text was chosen as an implement.

1. We are not concerned here with considering how the commentary text is more effective in handing down thought in comparison with any other text genre in Indian philosophy.

2.2 The Succession of Knowledge in Classical India

Let us consider the educational system in classical India under the following two aspects: the individual aspect and the organizational aspect, or, to put it more concretely, the methods of teaching between individuals and the institutions of teaching itself.

As for the individual aspect—the methods of teaching between individuals—it is clear that knowledge was handed down to students (pupils) from teachers. With regard to the relationship between students and teachers, especially the behavior of students toward teachers, the *Manusmṛti*, which provides the Hindu people guides for the details of life, gives us a few descriptions of the codes of student behavior toward teachers:[2]

> Both when ordered by his teacher, and without a (special) command, (a student) shall always exert himself in studying (the Veda), and in doing what is serviceable to his teacher.[3] (2–191)
>
> In the presence of his teacher let him always eat less, wear a less valuable dress and ornaments (than the former), and let him rise earlier (from his bed), and go to rest later.[4] (2–194)
>
> Wherever (people) justly censure or falsely defame his teacher, there he must cover his ears or depart thence to another place.[5] (2–200)
>
> By censuring (his teacher), though justly, he will become (in his next birth) an ass, by falsely defaming him, a dog; he who lives on his teacher's substance, will become a worm, and he who is envious (of his merit), a (larger) insect.[6] (2–201)

---

2. The translations of the *Manusmṛti* are quoted from Bühler [1886: 65–66]. Mazumder [1916: 121–123] and Watase [1991: 71–72] also offer a translation.
3. *Manusmṛti*, p. 423,26–27: *codito guruṇā nityam apracodita eva vā. kuryād adhyayane yogam ācāryasya hiteṣu ca.*
4. *Manusmṛti*, p. 426,6–7: *hīnānnavastraveṣaḥ syāt sarvadā gurusannidhau. uktiṣṭhet prathamaṃ cāsya caramaṃ caiva saṃviśet.*
5. *Manusmṛti*, p. 431,4–5: *guror yatra parīvādo nindā vāpi pravartate. karṇau tatra pidhātavyau gantavyaṃ vā tato 'nyataḥ.*
6. *Manusmṛti*, p. 431,22–23: *parīvādāt kharo bhavati śvā vai bhavati nindakaḥ. paribhoktā kṛmir bhavati kīṭo bhavati matsarī.*

From these descriptions we can see that an absolute obedience of students to their teachers was established and that knowledge was conveyed from teachers to students through this absolute obedience. One possible assumption from this is to conclude that students, in the learning environment, were not allowed to distinctly criticize or protest the authoritative thought taught by their authoritative teachers. If they had criticized or modified it, their conduct would have been regarded as a religious sin. Another possible assumption is that the learning environments limited a student's thinking to only this authoritative thought.[7] It is said that the relationship of absolute obedience between teacher and student was observed from the primary education level to the higher levels.[8]

Under the learning enviroments, education was mainly conducted through "oral lessons" in Sanskrit, and students had to duly memorize

---

7. The learning environments may have had an influence on forming the future of Indian philosophy. As Dasgupta [1997 (1922): 62–67], S. Chatterjee and D. Datta [1984 (1934): 9–12], and Raju [1985: 2–3] [1992: 37–38] have already shown in comparing the features of Indian philosophy by comparison with that of European philosophy, to summarize one clear and different feature between both philosophies, it is difficult to build the history of Indian philosophy from the viewpoint of the chronological development of a school and its theory in the manner in which the histories of European philosophy have been written. The reason for this is that Indian philosophy has not formed many new schools or new theories which deviate from the older schools or theories. Although it is a fact that two or more sub-schools have branched out from several schools of Indian philosophy, they did not come to establish independent schools. Moreover, even if a philosopher in ancient India enunciated a new idea, the new idea was generally regarded as an idea which had already been announced in the authoritative thought in order to maintain a school-founder's or elder teacher's authority. In the case of European philosophy, on the other hand, we can see that new and independent schools existed, and philosophers often enunciated new ideas without restrictions from the preceding thought. Consequently, it is possible to build the history of European philosophy by putting the schools or theories in chronological order.
8. The course of higher education began with upanayana, which is the initiation ceremony of a student being initiated to the Vedic study and entered upon studentship at the age of eight or ten. The normal duration of the course continued for twelve years. Those who wanted to become special experts had to continue for ten or twelve more years. In the course of the primary education which began at the age of five or six, before upanayana, the students studied alphabets, elementary arithmetic, and in the later stages of primary education, they studied Sanskrit grammar. Regarding this point, see C.K. Raja [1950: 78], Altekar [1951: 91–92, 153, 176–177], and Mitra [1964: 27].

these verbal teachings from the master. Of course not all knowledge was orally conveyed from teacher to student, with cases where it was conveyed through books.[9] However, instruction through books was not popular for twc main reasons. First, due to the rareness, costliness, and fragility of books, they were not easily available to the average student. Second, classical Indians had a prejudice against gaining knowledge from books.[10] This prejudice was derived from the method of the learning of the *Veda*s. The *Veda*s were prohibited from being written down by religious code, and in actual affairs, the proper accent and pronunciation in the Vedic recitation could only be correctly learned from oral teaching. The unwillingness to write down the *Veda*s seems to have had an influence on non-Vedic learning so that instruction through books was not popular, while, in general oral teaching seemed to be popular in many cases.[11]

Concerning the second organizational aspect regarding the institutions of teaching, it has been reported that public educational institutions like Buddhist monasteries, temple colleges, and Brāhmanic schools of Sanskrit learning flourished all over the land, mainly in the capitals of kingdoms and famous holy places. Cities such as Taxīla, Nālandā, Vikramashīla, Mithilā, and so forth were the great centers of education.[12] Students from distant cities flocked to these locations

---

9. As a proof, to begin with, it is reported that educational institutions like temple colleges and monasteries were organized as public educational institutions in ancient India. The educational institutions had library facilities that were not only for the storage of books but also for their publishers, and was where the copying work of manuscripts, for which the leaves of birch and palm were used, was done. See Altekar [1951: 77, 159], S.P. Chaube and A. Chaube [1999: 123, 143–146], and Scharfe [2002: 183–184]. To quote Altekar [1951: 157–158], "an author had to submit his work to a synod of scholars at a famous centre of learning like Pāṭalīputra or Benares, [...] it received its imprimateur which helped its acceptance and spread in provincial towns." In addition, Chinese Buddhist scholars such as I-tsing, who was in India between A.D. 673 and 685, went to India to study Sanskrit and Pāli and received true copies of the sacred texts of Buddhism. It shows from what has been said thus far that the teaching through the medium of books was also a method of instruction in ancient India.
10. For further details of the prejudice against gaining knowledge from books in ancient India, see Kane [1974: 347] and S.P. Chaube and A. Chaube [1999: 27].
11. Since such a way of learning presupposes the teacher's help, the way also might strengthen the absolute obedience of the teacher-student relationship.
12. Besides the cities previously mentioned, Valabhī, Odantpuri, Jagaddali, Nadia

for higher education and studied the *Veda*s, grammar, philosophy, etc. which were included in the curriculum of the educational institutions.[13]

From what has been said, we may sum up the educational system in classical India as follows: knowledge was mainly conveyed orally from generation to generation through the absolute obedience to the teacher-student relationship at the institutions of teaching.[14]

2.3 The Chain of the Indian Philosophic Text

In general, each school of Indian philosophy preserved and handed down its doctrine in the form of comment. In fact, several chains of commentaries, sub-commentaries, and sub-sub-commentaries on major texts are found in the philosophical schools. Chains typically begin with the *Sūtra*, attributed to the school founder. Hindu philosophical schools, for instance the Vaiśeṣika, the Vedānta, the Yoga, etc., have this basic *Sūtra* text, which is the source of doctrine in each school consisting of a set of brief and significant aphorisms (*sūtra*s) that do not elaborate on the doctrine. The reason for this is that the brief expression of the *Sūtra* is suitable for memorization of the doctrine by those who already have knowledge of the doctrine by virtue of being given oral instruction about it. While the *Sūtra* has a function of helping memorization of the doctrine, it also has authority as a sacred book of the school on the grounds that the school founder wrote it. Therefore, the thought of the *Sūtra* was regarded as *authoritative* thought, and scholars succeeding after the founders paid high esteem and respect to the *Sūtra*.

---

were also important educational centers. See Mazumder [1916: 89–100], Keay [1918: 49–57], Altekar [1951: 105–143], and S.P. Chaube and A. Chaube [1999: 137–151].

13. We have no definite information on how philosophical schools such as the Vedānta and the Vaiśeṣika came to be established and existed. However, what has to be noted is that students selected one of the doctrines of philosophy for specialization by their own choice in the curriculum of public educational institutions. According to Altekar [1951: 92, 153, 157], at the age of thirteen or fourteen, after finishing the grammar course in five or six years, students selected one of the subjects like logic, philosophy, poetics astronomy, and mathematics for specialization.
14. Although we lack definite information on how knowledge was conveyed from place to place, it may be safe to assume that open forums held in public places played an important role in the academic world in ancient India with regard to the spread of knowledge. See Bronkhorst [2010].

Accompanying this, the text genre called the *Bhāṣya*, which is a commentary on the *Sūtra*, contains explanation and interpretation of unclear meaning of aphorisms in the *Sūtra*. Therefore the *Bhāṣya* might have been useful for those who had not been given sufficient oral instruction on the *Sūtra* to understand it. In turn, the text genre called the *Ṭīkā*, which is a commentary on the *Bhāṣya*, makes a detailed description of this *Bhāṣya*. The main reason why the genre of the *Ṭīkā* is made is the occurrence of attacks by other rival schools regarding doctrine. This would also apply to the case of the *Bhāṣya*. To establish the superiority of the doctrine to which the commentators adhere, commentators had to answer to these objections. As we shall see later in section 2.5 in this Chapter, we can consider this progress of controversy between the commentator and the opponent through the consideration of the *Ṭīkā*.[15]

Through this medium of the text genre called the *Sūtra*, the *Bhāṣya*, and the *Ṭīkā*, a doctrine was carried out in a school. It must be noted here that although there is a single *Sūtra*, there are cases where there are more than one *Bhāṣya* and *Ṭīkā*. That is to say, diverse and multiple interpretations were composed for the *Sūtra* in the form of the *Bhāṣya* and were applied to the *Bhāṣya* in the form of the *Ṭīkā*. Viewed in a different light, it has been shown that there were two or more interpretations to an authoritative thought, which stems from the *Sūtra* directly or indirectly in the form of the *Bhāṣya* and the *Ṭīkā*.[16]

2.4 The Communication Theory

Before considering the system of the commentary text from a viewpoint of communication theory, let us discuss first of all the communication theory itself. Basic communication consists of four elements: a sender, code(s), a message, and a receiver. With these elements having relevance to each other, communication materializes. The process of

---

15. The explanation of such text genres as the *Sūtra*, the *Bhāṣya*, and the *Ṭīkā* is more fully developed in Dasgupta [1997 (1922): 62–67], S. Chatterjee and D. Datta [1984 (1934): 10–12], Coward (ed.) [1996 (1983): 7 8], and Raju [1985: 35–36].
16. Although this now raises the question of what the authoritative thought for the commentators was and how a commentator considered other commentaries on the same material, it is not necessary for the purpose of this chapter to enter into a detailed discussion of these questions.

this materialization is as follows: the sender converts or symbolizes his thought into a message while making reference to a code. The message must be shown with a discernible form for a receiver. The receiver then decodes the message while making reference to the same code, and understands the thought of the sender.[17] The term "code(s)" is defined as "a shared set of rules or CONVENTIONS by which SIGNS can be combined to permit a message to be communicated from one person to another."[18] We can give it elements, such as grammar, vocabulary, etc. We can also represent the process of communication diagrammatically as in the following Figure 1:[19]

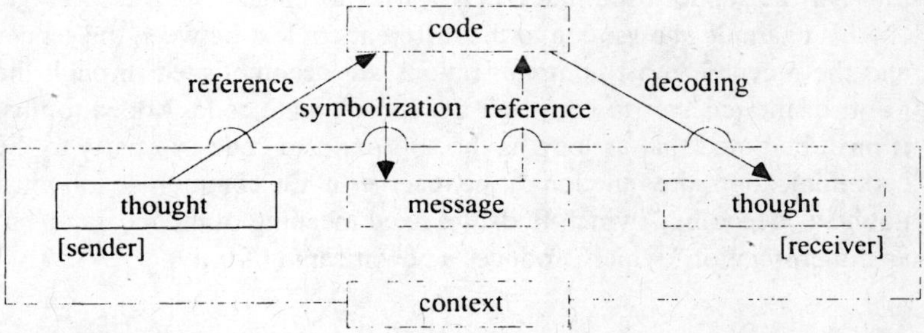

Figure 1

As Figure 1 indicates, *ideal* communication materializes when both the sender and the receiver refer to the same code. If the receiver reads the message referring to a code that is different than the sender's, his understanding of the message would not be perfect, or if worst comes to worst, he would not be able to decode it at all. As a result, the communication would come to be imperfect or collapse.

However, most communications actually are far from ideal in the sense that both the sender and the receiver cannot help referring to different codes. Since there is more or less a gap of space and time between both (we may rephrase "a gap of space and time" into

---

17. Regarding the framework and its process of the communication, see Jakobson [2003 (1973): 188] and C.E. Shannon and W. Weaver [1969: 14].
18. See Baldick [2001 (1990): 43].
19. Ikegami [1997 (1984): 39] made use of a diagram in order to explain the process of communication. Ikegami's diagram has been altered in this figure.

"different context"), the possibility that both of them refer to the same code is weak or rare. To take an example, a reader (the receiver) may come across unintelligible sentences (the message) in classical foreign literature. The lack of understanding of the sentences is often due to the fact that the reader does not refer to the same code as the author (the sender) did. Since there is, in this case, a great gap of space and time between the reader and the author, the reader cannot refer to the same code as the author did, so that he can only guess the probable meaning of the sentences from the approximate code which the author referred to.[20] That is to say, inferring the code that the sender referred to, namely, referring to the code composed of nothing but approximations of what the sender used, the receiver tries to understand the message. As this example shows, due to the different context between the sender and the receiver, most communications are accomplished through the effort of the receiver to construct the approximate code. Added to this, it must be noted that as long as the approximate code is a party to the communication, the function of the receiver in the communication must not be a "decoding," which finds the fixed meaning of the message, but an "interpretation" which produces a new meaning for it.

2.5 Analysis of the Commentary Text

Let us then attempt to apply this communication theory to the Indian Philosophic commentary text, concentrating on the *Ṭīkā* (the commentary text) on the *Bhāṣya* (the original text).[21] When applying this communication theory, we can find that the commentary text consists of two types of communication: the first is between the author of the original text (the author of the *Bhāṣya*) and a commentator (the author of the *Ṭīkā*); the second is between the opponent and the commentator. First, we will explain the former. Of the four elements of communication, the sender is the author of the original text, the message is the original text, the receiver is the commentator, and the code consists of the doctrines on which both the author of the original

20. Useful information on the communication theory is contained in the Ikegami [1997 (1984): 35–64].

21. The *Sūtra* is the original text for the *Bhāṣya* and the *Bhāṣya* is the original text for the *Ṭīkā*. When I speak of "the original text" in this book, I mean a text on which the commentary text makes comment.

text and the commentator are dependent, the Sanskrit grammar, vocabulary, etc. The process of communication can be schematized as in the following Figure 2:

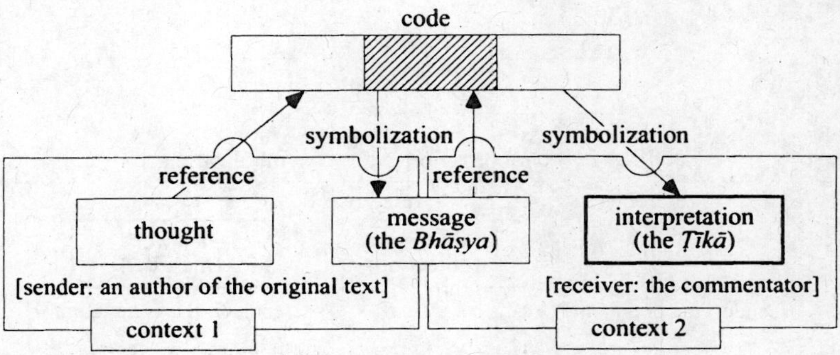

Figure 2

The author of the original text symbolizes his thought into the *Bhāṣya* (message) while making reference to the code. The commentator (the receiver) understands partly the *Bhāṣya* while making reference to the code.[22] Then, the commentator symbolizes his idea of the *Bhāṣya* into the interpretation (the *Ṭīkā*) while making reference to the code. Regarding the code, the author of the original text and the commentator refer to different codes from each other, although both have some codes in common which are designated in the crosshatched area of Figure 2. The reason for this is that if both referred to the same code, the original text and the commentary text would have no difference in expressions and content. However, in fact there is a difference between them. Therefore the codes referrenced by both come to be different, and the commentary text itself comes to be a manifestation of the "interpretation" of the original text.

Turning now to the latter communication between the opponent and the commentator. Of the four elements of communication: the sender is the opponents, the message is their objections, the receiver is

22. There is a different context between the author of original text and the commentator, so that the commentator could only guess the probable meaning of the *Bhāṣya* from the approximate code. Namely, his understanding of it would not be perfect. See section 2.4 in this Chapter.

the commentator, and the code consists of the doctrines on which each one of the opponents and the commentator are dependent, Sanskrit grammar, vocabulary, etc. The process of communication can be schematized as in the following Figure 3:

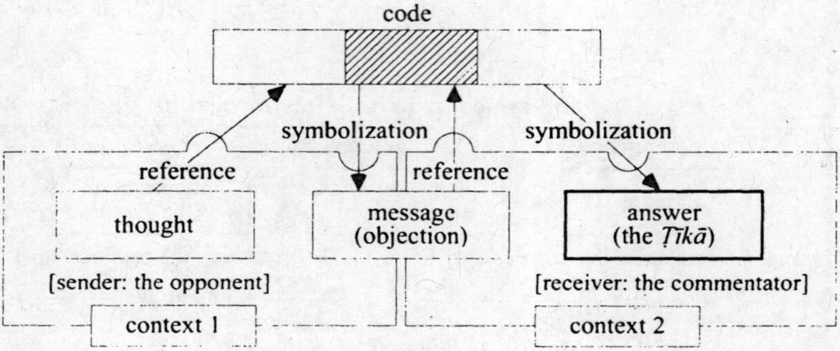

Figure 3

The opponent (the sender) symbolizes his thoughts into the objection (message) while making reference to the code.[23] The commentator (the receiver) understands, in part, the objections while making reference to a similar version of the code. Then, the commentator symbolizes his idea of the objection into an answer (the *Ṭīkā*) while making reference to the code.[24] In this case also, the reference codes of the opponent and of the commentator are not the same. If the codes were the same, in principle, the opponent would not raise an objection to the doctrine on which the commentator depends, or the commentator would accept the objections.[25] In this way, the commentary text is of a manifestation of

23. The opponents offer the counterargument from the standpoint of their doctrine, showing a logical defect in the rival's doctrine. Although there is a case where the counterargument is traced back to the opponent's text, there is no conclusive proof whether the counterargument was actually offered by opponents or not. One possibility is to assume that it was made through a self-question by the author himself.
24. The answer points out the defect and logical mismatching of the counterargument, and proves that the counterargument is not valid. And finally, the justification of its own doctrine is asserted.
25. The recurrence of the counterargument from opponents, and the answer to the counterargument on any philosophical subject in turn, is in the text, and the argument is continuous. Regarding the dialogic form in the text, Fillizat

the "answer" to the counterargument through the above process.[26]

Now we can recognize from what has been said thus far that the commentary text (the *Ṭīkā*) is of two aspects: the manifestation of "interpretation" and that of an "answer." which are respectively indicated in the areas within the thick lines in Figure 2 and Figure 3. However, it must be noted that both of these aspects do not appear separately in the commentary text. In other words, both cannot be separately extracted. Both are what appeared and resulted from having applied communication theory to the commentary text. Moreover, the important point is that the two aspects—"interpretation" and "answer"—exist with reciprocal action. To be more explicit, when the commentator makes an "interpretation" of the original text, he needs to show the "interpretation" which eludes the points of the counterargument that shows the logical defect in the doctrine on which the commentator is dependent. And the "answer" to the counterargument contains a clear demonstration of the counterargument's invalidity. Accordingly, when the "interpretation" of the original text is generated, it comes to be under the influence of the "answer" to the counterargument.[27]

[1975: 173] reports that the *Mahābhāṣya* of Patañjari (150 B.C.), which is a commentary upon the *Aṣṭādhyāyī*, is the first text that includes the dialogic form, and that the *Mahābhāṣya* has become the model of the style and the reasoning in the history of Sanskrit literature. However, the dialogic form is not unique to the composition of the commentary but can be found in other text genres as well. In addition to the *Śūtra*, the *Bhāṣya*, and the *Ṭīkā*, there are also independent texts on the doctrines called the *Kārikā* and the *Vārttika*. The former summarizes the important topics of any doctrine in a succinct manner; the latter makes an observation on any doctrine in verses. This point is more fully explained by Dasgupta [1997 (1922): 67].

26. We can see this process in the text, to be concrete, the dialogic form can be found in the text. The dialogic form is shown in clear form in the Sanskrit syntax. The expression "if it is objected that [...]" (*atha ... iti cet*) is a typical example. After an expression of objection, the reply, for example, "it (the objection) is not true because [...]." (*tat na, ... -tvāt.* or *tat na, hi....*), follows it. In this case, we can clearly find the dialogic form in the expression. This dialogic form in the text seems to reflect a way of learning at the educational institutions of those days. Debate and discussion were used as devices of learning, and the students were required to have the ability of defending their own ideas and defeating those of their opponents in discussion. See Keay [1918: 53, 101], Altekar [1951: 164, 167], S.P. Chaube and A. Chaube [1999: 100, 118], and Bronkhorst [2010].

27. The original text only gives the commentator fragmentary knowledge of the

On the other hand, the "interpretation" of the original text also has an influence on the "answer" to the counterargument. The reasons for this are that the "answer" must be made in accordance with the doctrine of the school, and that the doctrine, which the commentator holds valid, is declared in his "interpretation" of the *Bhāṣya*. Even if the answer has successfully responded to the counterargument, it would not be effective in a case where the contents of the answer deviate from the doctrine. Therefore when the "answer" to the counterargument is generated, it comes to be under the influence of the "interpretation." From this viewpoint, one may say that the commentary text has a system in which the two aspects interact with each other—the influence of the "answer" to the counterargument on the "interpretation" of the original text, and the influence of the "interpretation" on the "answer."

2.6 The System of Commentary Text from the Communication Theory

Applying communication theory to the commentary text in Indian philosophy, we find that the commentary text is composed of two types of communication to which the commentator is a party as the receiver. One is with the author of the original text, the other with the opponent. This application also makes the commentary text manifest two aspects of itself, the "interpretation" of the original text and the "answer" to the counterargument. The interaction between these two aspects composes the system of the commentary text. That is to say, when the "interpretation" is generated, the "answer" evokes an influence on it. On the other hand, when the "answer" is generated, the "interpretation" creates an influence on it. Viewed in this light, the key to success in communication is dependent upon another communication, and success in both forms of communication results in the contents of the commentary text gaining validity.

This idea of the system of the commentary text helps account for

---

doctrine for answering the counterargument, since the opponents show the objections which take a shot at the unresolved or unwritten philosophical subjects in the original text. Therefore, the commentator needs to give careful consideration of the counterargument each time he interprets the original text. That is to say, he makes efforts to interpret the original text while resolving the problems that its opponents point out. This is the influence of the "answer" on the "interpretation."

the reason why the commentary text was chosen as a main implement of communication in classical Indian philosophy. As we have assumed, the religious sin covers the criticism or modification of authoritative thought. However, it is impossible for this authoritative thought to be transcendental and inviolable in nature since it cannot escape from the influence of counterargument. That is to say, it is updated each time a commentary act occurs by virtue of the counterargument. In this sense, the commentary act involves committing the religious sin. The authoritative thought must be reformed in order to continuously preserve and reassert this authority. The commentary text provides an effective system for reforming the authoritative thought without asking the commentator to undergo the deadly sin of direct criticism or modification since it is not the commentator but the system of commentary texts that inevitably reforms this authoritative thought through criticism. Thus, it is possible to suppose that the commentary text was selected as a medium for conveying knowledge in classical India because of its ability to allow for this surreptitious change and adjustment without finding out who is responsible for it.

Chapter 3

Originality and Quotation

3.1 Introduction

In Chapter 3, we analyze the genesis of commentary texts in classical Indian philosophy from a viewpoint of quotation theory in order to show an aspect of generative system of the commentary text. Allow me to summarize the main points that will be made in this chapter. Taking the concept of quotation into consideration, we will focus detailed attention on the way in which information is quoted or drawn from the precedent commentary texts. To be more explicit, the way of quotation will be roughly divided into two types, explicit quotation and implicit quotation; furthermore the former will be classified into four forms. On the basis of this manner of quotation, the genesis of commentary texts will be analyzed. Added to this, a social context, which contributes to the genesis of commentary texts, will also be offered. We will then show with an explanation for this process itself, that is to say, the commentary texts in classical India are generated via combination with already-known information, and that they are of a character of the texture of quotation (or "a mosaic of citations").[1]

For this consideration, I, again, utilize the definition of "inherence" (*samavāya*) chapter of the *Vyomavatī* (*Vy*) by Vyomaśiva (ca. 900–960), the *Nyāyakandalī* (*NK*) by Śrīdhara (ca. 950–1000), and the *Kiraṇāvalī* (*Kir*) by Udayana (ca. 1050–1100), which are commentary from medieval India on the *Padārthadharmasaṃgraha* (*PDhS*) by Praśastapāda (ca. 550–600). Using these three commentary texts, we will consider how the commentators made commentaries on

---

1. See Kristeva [1969: 85], "*tout texts se construit comme mosaïque de citations, tout texte est absorption et tranformation d'un autre texte.*"

inherence's definition in the *PDhS* and, subsequently, one aspect of genesis of Indian philosophic commentary texts themselves from the viewpoint of quotation theory.

3.2 Inherence's Definition in the *PDhS*

The *PDhS* defines "inherence" as follows:

> That which is the relation, being a cause of the idea "[this is] here (this is in that)," between entities that fix without being separate [from each other], which [stand as] the superstratum and the substratum, is inherence.
> (*PDhS*, no. 9: *ayutasiddhānām ādhāryādhārabhūtānaṃ yaḥ sambandha ihapratyayahetuḥ sa samavāyaḥ.*)

The preceding definition of inherence may be separated into four factors or parts:

(I) entities that fix without being separate [from each other] (*ayutasiddha*),
(II) entities that [stand as] the superstratum and the substratum (*ādhāryādhārabhūta*),
(III) the relation (*sambandha*), and
(IV) a cause of the idea "[this is] here" (*ihapratyayahetu*).

First of all, we have to consider the role of "definition" itself, since this inquiry must give us a proper way of analyzing this definition. The role of a definition may be simply stated as "the decision of the meaning of a word, sign, or concept." However, a definition is not perfect when it is also applied to the meanings of other words, signs, or concepts not explicitly defined. Accordingly, if a definition is composed of several words, each word of the definition has a function that prevents the whole definition from applying to these other words and entities that do not fit the particular meaning of the defined.[2] In other words, a definition *defines* the meaning of the defined object through the exclusion of other objects. On the basis of this view, we will take a close look at what each of the three commentary texts on the *PDhS* excludes by their chosen factor of inherence's definition of the

2. On the consideration of the function of definitions in Indian philosophy, see Matilal [1990 (1985): 176–202] and Sato [1995].

PDhS; as, for example, the *Vy* excludes "the relation between a bowl and a fruit of jujube" by factor (I). This will lead us to a discussion of how the commentary texts are generated. It is also this exploration of the understanding of the *PDhS*'s definition of inherence by the commentators that might offer a useful insight into this particular implement of communication. I will outline these points based on the order from the *Vy*.

3.3 What is Excluded by Each Factor of the Definition of Inherence in the Commentary Texts

3.3.1 The *Vy*

The *Vy* first supposes that the definition of inherence is only composed of factor (IV)—That which is a cause of the idea "[this is] here" (*ihapratyayahetu*) is inherence. However, this definition cannot exclude "the village and the trees (the forest)," since both of them cause the idea "the trees are in the village" and technically fits factor (IV). Therefore, factor (III)—the relation (*sambandha*)—is added to the definition composed of (IV) only in order to exclude them from the concept of inherence. When a man sees a village and the trees from a distance, although both of them are far from each other, he has the idea "the trees are in the village" by virtue of an imaginary relation between them. That is to say, in this case, there is in fact no relation between the village and the trees, since an intermediate space[3] actually occurs between them. Therefore, even if they cause the idea "the trees are in the village," they are excluded from the concept of inherence by virtue of factor (III).[4]

However, even if the definition is composed of (III) and (IV)—That which is the relation, being a cause of the idea "[this is] here," is inherence—there is still a deviation from the concept of inherence by virtue of "the relation between the ether and a [flying] bird," since this relation causes the idea "[this flying] bird is in the ether" and comes to fit the definition composed of (III) and (IV) only. In turn, in

---

3. Regarding the concept of "an intermediate space" (*antarāla*), see fn. 3 in the translation of the *Vy* in Part II.
4. See section [1] "The relation (*sambandha*)" in the translation of the *Vy* in Part II.

order to prevent this deviation, factor (II)—entities that [stand as] the superstratum and the substratum (*ādhāryādhārabhūta*)—must be added to the definition. According to the *Vy*, since "the relation between the ether and a [flying] bird" is regarded as that between the pervading (the ether) and the pervaded (a flying bird), the ether, which is a pervasive entity, cannot only be regarded as the substratum but also as the superstratum for a [flying] bird. And therefore, "the relation between the ether and a [flying] bird" is excluded from the concept of inherence by the addition of factor (II).[5]

For an objection that cognition of "[this is] here" does not occur for the ether since the ether is beyond the senses and the cognition of "here" can only occur to an object that is grasped by a sense of organ, the *Vy* replies that the cognition of "[this is] here" for the ether does occurs, although it is illusion. In order to exclude this illusionary cognition of "here" for the ether indirectly, factor (II) is there. Moreover, to exclude the illusionary cognition "the trees are in the village" for the village and the trees, factor (III) is there.[6]

Moreover, to this definition, composed of (II), (III), and (IV)— That which is the relation, being a cause of the idea "[this is] here," between entities that [stand as] the superstratum and the substratum, is inherence—factor (I)—entities that fix without being separate [from each other] (*ayutasiddha*)—must be added for the purpose of excluding "the relation between a bowl and a fruit of jujube" from the concept of inherence. We can illustrate the structure of this relation in Figure 1.[7]

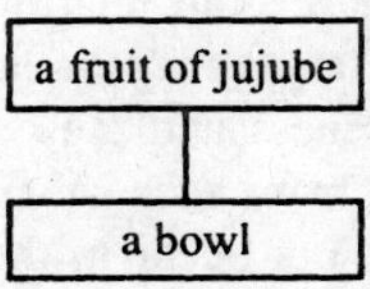

Figure 1

According to Vaiśeṣika philosophy, this relation is "conjunction

5. See section [2.1] "The relation between the ether and a [flying] bird" in the translation of the *Vy* in Part II.
6. See section [2.2] "The cognition of 'here' for the ether and the relation (*sambandha*)—1" and [2.3] "The cognition of 'here' for the ether and the relation (*sambandha*)—2" in the translation of the *Vy* in Part II.
7. Regarding the detailed explanation of the system of the diagrams, see Chapter 1.

(*saṃyoga*)," subsisting between entities that fix separately (*yutasiddha*). However, the definition of inherence, composed of (II), (III), and (IV) only, cannot exclude "the relation between a bowl and a fruit of jujube." Because the fruit of jujube and the bowl stand as the superstratum and the substratum respectively (II), there is a relation between the bowl and the fruit of jujube (III), and this relation causes the idea that "the fruit of jujube is in the bowl" (IV). Therefore, if the definition of "inherence" is only composed of factor (II), (III), and (IV), "the relation between a bowl and a fruit of jujube" will come to be inherence. For the purpose of excluding this relation from the concept of inherence, the *Vy* argues that factor (I)—entities that fix without being separate [from each other] (*ayutasiddha*)—must also be added to the definition.[8]

To backtrack slightly, and look at this from another example, if inherence is defined using only (I) and (III)—That which is the relation between entities that fix without separate [from each other] is inherence—it will be applicable to the cases "the relation of the denoted and the denoter (*vācyavācakabhāva*)," and "that of an object and the cognition of the object (*viṣayaviṣayibhāva*)."[9] The *Vy* provides specific relations under both of these cases as well; "the relation of largeness (*mahattva*) in the ether and the articulated word 'largeness' (*mahattvaśabda*) for largeness in the ether," under the former case, and "the relation of desire (*icchā*) in a soul and consciousness of desire (*icchālambanavijñāna*) in the soul," under the latter. We can illustrate the structure of both of these relations in Figures 2 and 3.

Now, the definition composed of factor (I) and (III) is not sufficient to exclude the case "the relation of largeness in the ether and the articulated word 'largeness' for largeness in the ether." The reason for this is that largeness and the articulated word "largeness" fix without being separate from each other in the sense that separate existence (*yutasiddhi*) does not occur in them. That is to say, they do not have different loci respectively, but have the same locus (the ether) (I), and a relation occurs between them as one of the denoted and the denoter (III). If the definition of inherence is only composed of factor (I) and (III) "the relation of largeness in the ether and the articulated

8. See section [3] "Entities that fix without being separate [from each other] (*ayutasiddha*)" in the translation of the *Vy* in Part II.
9. With regard to *viṣayaviṣayibhāva*, see fn. 21 in the translation of the *Vy* in Part II..

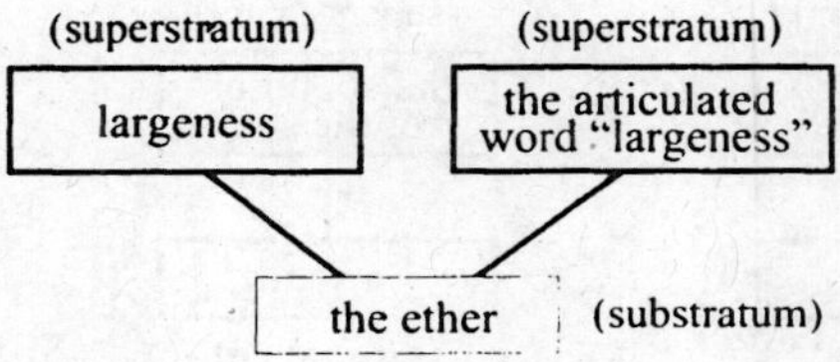

Figure 2

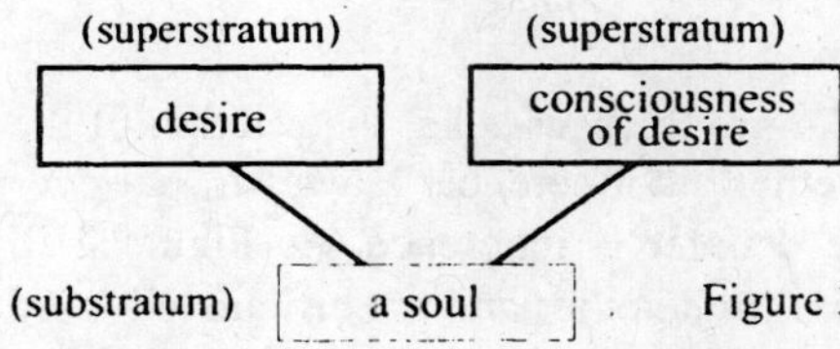

Figure 3

word 'largeness' for largeness in the ether" will not be excluded from its concept. Therefore, factor (II)—entities that [stand as] the superstratum and the substratum (*ādhāryādhārabhūta*)—needs to be added to the definition for the purpose of excluding the above relation from the concept of inherence. Since largeness and the articulated word "largeness" do not stand as the superstratum and the substratum, factor (II) can exclude the relation from the concept of inherence. For the same reasons mentioned above, "the relation of desire in a soul and consciousness of desire in the soul," under the relation of an object and the cognition of the object, is also excluded from the concept of inherence by factor (II).[10]

Again, even though the definition composed of (I), (II), and (III)—That which is the relation between entities that fix without being separate [from each other], which [stand as] the superstratum and the substratum, is inherence—it is still applicable to "the relation of the denoted and the denoter" and to "that of an object and the cognition of the object." The *Vy* again provides specific relations under both of these cases; the relation of the ether (*ākāśa*) and the articulated word "ether" (*ākāśaśabda*), under the former case, and the relation of a soul (*ātman*) and the cognition of the soul (*ātmālambanajñāna*), under the latter. We can illustrate the structure of both relations in Figures 4 and 5.

10. See section [4.1] "The relation of the denoted and the denoter, and that of an object and the cognition of the object—1" in the translation of the *Vy* in Part II.

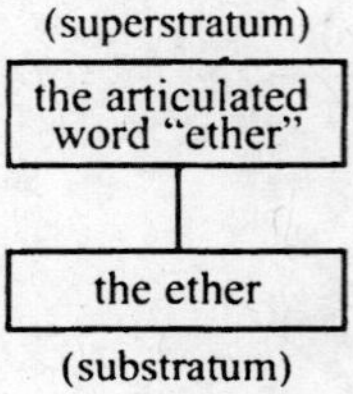

Figure 4

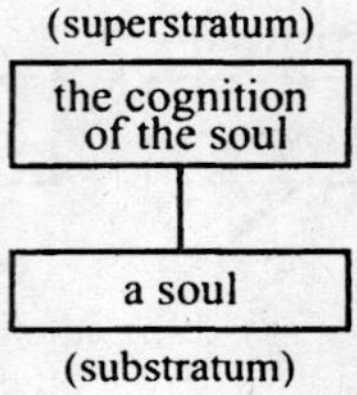

Figure 5

According to the Vaiśeṣika, the relation of the ether and the articulated word "ether" is inherence. However, not every relation of the denoted and the denoter is inherence. As Figure 2 illustrates, "the relation of largeness in the ether and the articulated word 'largeness' for largeness in the ether," under the relation of the denoted and the denoter, is not inherence. The same is true of the relation of an object and the cognition of the object on the evidence of "the relation of desire in a soul and consciousness of desire in the soul" in Figure 3. Therefore, the *Vy* insists that factor (II) must be interpreted as "*only* entities that stand as the superstratum and the substratum." The interpretation of factor (II) with this restriction[11] serves to exclude both cases[12]—the relation of the denoted and the denoter, and that of an object and the cognition of the object—from the concept of inherence since both may or may not subsist between entities that stand as the superstratum and the substratum.[13]

Moreover, the *Vy* interprets factor (I) as "*only* entities that fix without being separate [from each other]." By virtue of the interpretation of (I), with the restriction of the word "only," the relation of the denoted and the denoter and that of an object and the cognition of the object come to be swept away from the concept of inherence, since both cases emphasize relations which do not always subsist between entities that fix without being separate from each other. Although the *Vy* does not provide specific relations for both cases, we can construct examples for both cases that do not subsist between entities that fix

11. Regarding the function of "only" (*eva*) in Indian philosophy, see Kajiyama [1966].
12. The narrow application (*avyāpti*) of the definition of inherence is pointed out. Regarding this point, see fn. 33 in the translation of the *Vy* in Part II.
13. See section [4.2] "The relation of the denoted and the denoter, and that of an object and the cognition of the object—2" in the translation of the *Vy* in Part II.

without being separate from each other. For example, the relation of a pot and the articulated word "pot," under the relation of the denoted and the denoter, and the relation of a pot and the cognition of the pot, under the relation of an object and the cognition of the object.[14] We can illustrate the structure of both relations in Figures 6 and 7.

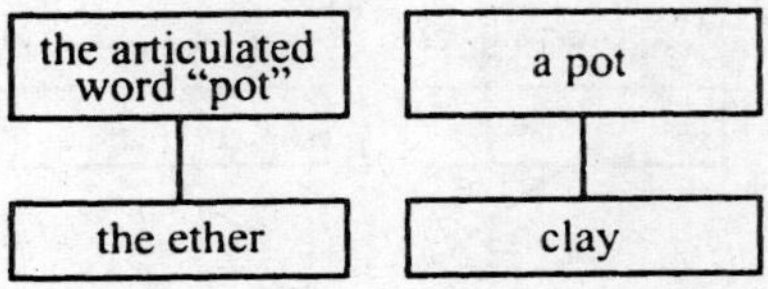

Figure 6

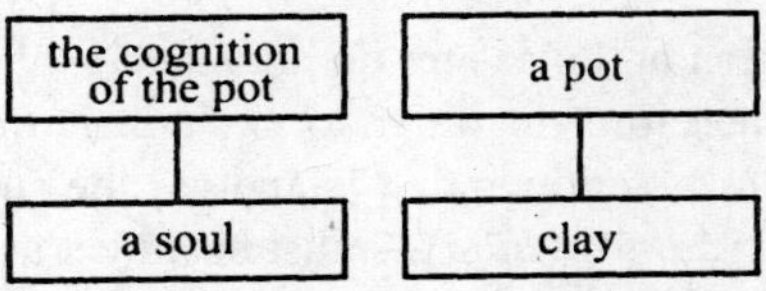

Figure 7

Accordingly, the interpretation of factor (I), which explicitly says that inherence subsists between *only* entities that fix without being separate [from each other], serves to exclude the relation of the denoted and the denoter and that of an object and its cognition, since both relations may or may not subsist between entities that fix without being separate from each other.[15]

3.3.2 The *NK*

Second we will consider this same process in the *NK*, focusing on what is excluded by its handling of the factors of the inherence's definition. The *NK* first supposes that the definition of inherence is composed of factor (I) and (III)—the relation between entities that fix without being separate [from each other] (*ayutasiddha*) is inherence. In this case, "the relation of merit and pleasure" could reasonably be understood as inherence, since merit and pleasure, which are examples

14. With regard to the relations for both cases that subsist between entities that fix without being separate from each other, see Figure 2 and Figure 3, and Figure 4 and Figure 5.
15. See section [5.1] "Addition of a restriction (*eva*) to *ayutasiddha*" in the translation of the *Vy* in Part II.

of qualities,[16] are also entities that fix without being separate from each other in the sense that separate existence (*yutasiddhi*) does not occur in them. That is to say, both merit and pleasure do not have different loci respectively, but have the state of sharing a locus (soul) with the other (*sāmānādhikaraṇya*). We can illustrate the structure of the aforementioned case in Figure 8.

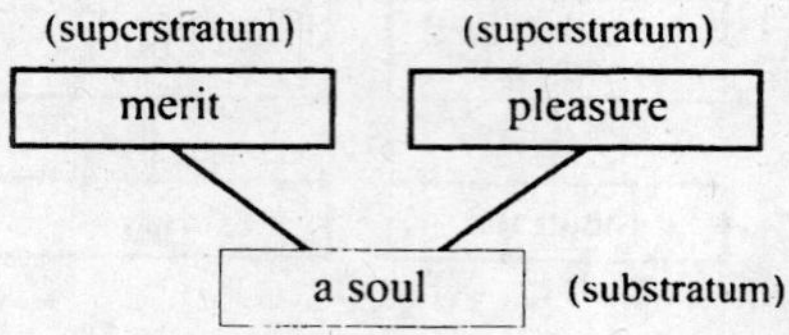

Figure 8

The relation of merit and pleasure do not stand as the superstratum and the substratum, therefore, in order to exclude it from the concept of inherence, factor (II)—entities that [stand as] the superstratum and the substratum (*ādhāryādhārabhūta*)—must be added to the definition.[17]

Next the *NK* deals with "the relation between the ether and a [flying] bird" and insists that the relation be excluded by factor (I) without giving a detailed explanation, commenting that factor (II) does not have a role of excluding this relation.[18] It should be noted that the *Vy* and the *NK* disagree regarding this "relation between the ether and a [flying] bird," where the *Vy* interprets the relation as explicitly excluded by factor (II).[19]

Moreover, the *NK* deals with "the relation of the denoted and the denoter," for which the specific relation is the relation of the ether (the denoted) and the articulated word "ether" (the denoter). We have already illustrated the structure of this relation in Figure 4. The *NK* argues that factor (IV)—a cause of the idea "[this is] here" (*ihapratyayahetu*)—is included in the definition in order to exclude "the relation of the denoted and the denoter" from the concept of

16. See section 1.2 "The Vaiśeṣika Categories" in Chapter 1.
17. See section [2.1] "The relation of merit and pleasure" in the translation of the *NK* in Part III.
18. See section [2.2] "The relation between the ether and a [flying] bird" in the translation of the *NK* in Part III.
19. See section [2.1] "The relation between the ether and a [flying] bird" in the translation of the *Vy* in Part II.

inherence, since this relation does not cause the idea "[this is] here."[20]

Even if the definition is only composed of (II), (III), and (IV)—[the relation], being a cause of the idea that "[this is] here," between entities that [stand as] the superstratum and the substratum is inherence[21]—it is still applicable to "the relation between a bowl and a fruit of jujube." However, this relation is conjunction (*saṃyoga*), not inherence. Therefore, the *NK* insists that factor (I)—entities that fix without being separate [from each other]—must be included in the definition in order to exclude this relation from the concept of inherence.[22]

3.3.3 The *Kir*

Finally, we will consider the *Kir*. The *Kir* analyzes factor (I)—entities that fix without being separate [from each other] (*ayutasiddha*)—as "these [entities] are not only inseaprate (*ayuta*) [or] connected (*prāpta*), but also fixed (*siddha*)." The relation between these entities is understood as inherence which is of a character of connection (*prāpti*).[23] And Factor (I), which touches on such a conception, excludes "conjunction" from the concerned relation, since "conjunction" is preceded by non-connection.[24]

Moreover, the *Kir* deals with the relation of the denoted and the denoter etc., and insists that the relation be excluded by factor (II)—entities that [stand as] the superstratum and the substratum (*ādhāryādhārabhūta*). The reason for this is that the relation of the denoted and the denoter occurs by an accidental attribute, while the relation of the superstratum and the substratum occurs naturally.[25]

---

20. See section [3] "A cause of the idea '[this is] here' (*ihapratyayahetu*)" in the translation of the *NK* in Part III.
21. Although this constructed inherence's definition does not contain factor (III), the relation (*sambandha*), in the text, Śrīdhara might readily have assumed the definition which contains factor (III). Otherwise, the constructed definition would not be applicable the *relation* between a bowl and a fruit of jujube.
22. See section [4.1] "The relation between a bowl and a fruit of jujube" in the translation of the *NK* in Part III.
23. See section [1.1] "Consideration of *ayutasiddha*" in the translation of the *Kir* in Part IV.
24. See section [1.2] "The relation of conjunction (*saṃyoga*)" in the translation of the *Kir* in Part IV.
25. See section [2] "Entities that [stand as] the superstratum and the substratum (*ādhāryādhārabhūta*)" in the translation of the *Kir* in Part IV.

3.4 Quotation Theory

The exclusions related to each factor (part) of the definition of inherence in the three commentary texts are summarized in table I:

Table I: What is excluded by the factors of the definition of inherence

	The *Vy*	The *NK*	The *Kir*
(I)	1. The relation between a bowl and a fruit of jujube (=Conjunction) 2. The relation of the denoted and the denoter (* The relation of a pot and the articulated word "pot") 3. The relation of an object and the cognition of the object (* The relation of a pot and the cognition of the pot)	1. The relation between the ether and a [flying] bird 2. The relation between a bowl and a fruit of jujube	1. Conjunction
(II)	1. The relation between the ether and a [flying] bird 2. The relation of the denoted and the denoter <a> The relation of largeness in the ether and the articulated word "largeness" for largeness in the ether <b> The relation of the ether and the articulated word "ether" 3. The relation of an object and the cognition of the object <a> The relation of desire in a soul and consciousness of desire in the soul <b> The relation of a soul and the cognition of the soul	1. The relation of merit and pleasure	1. The relation of the denoted and the denoter etc.

(III)	1. The trees (forest) and the village		
(IV)		1. The relation of the denoted and the denoter <a> The relation of the ether and the articulated word "ether"	

(I) entities that fix without being separate [from each other] (*ayutasiddha*), (II) entities that [stand as] the superstratum and the substratum (*ādhāryādhārabhūta*), (III) the relation (*sambandha*), (IV) a cause of the idea "[this is] here" (this is in that) (*ihapratyayahetu*).
What is excluded with * in table II is not referred to in the text.

In the preceding chapter we observed numerous examples of the combination of the definition factors, and what is excluded (the exclusion), between the three commentary texts. Let us now discuss this genesis of commentary texts from the perspective of quotation theory, considering how the commentary texts are generated via combination with already-known information—both the factors of definition and what is excluded—which are quoted from the preceding texts. This allows us to focus attention on the way in which information is quoted from precedent texts and subsequently manipulated.

The term "quotation" can be simply defined as information in a precedent text moved to a subsequent text, implicitly or explicitly. Therefore, "quotation" may be divided into two types: explicit quotation and implicit quotation.[26] Further, explicit quotation can occur in the form of "the preservation," the "substitution," and the "permutation" of information between texts. And in each of these cases we can perceive the movement of information from the precedent text to the following text. On the other hand, implicit quotation takes the form of the "deletion" of information between texts, where we cannot perceive the movement of information from the precedent text to the following.

The above can be schematized as follows:

26. With regard to the concept of quotation, see Sasaki [1990] and Matsuzawa [2003: 27–29]. However the concept of quotation, which is offered in this chapter, is not explained in their papers.

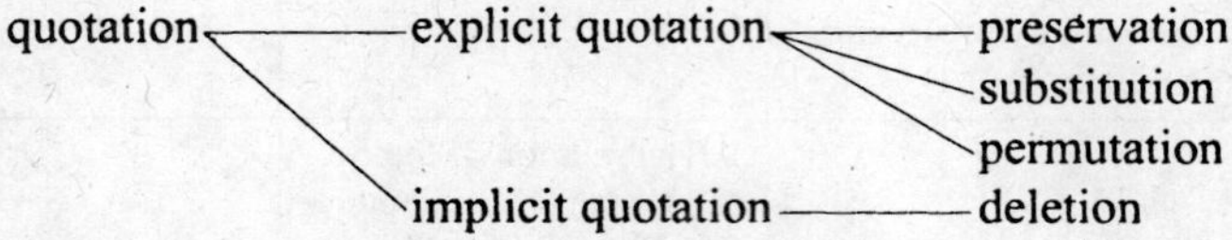

Having made this distinction, we shall explain each a kind of quotation with the combination of the definition factors (x and y) and what is excluded (a, b, and c) between the commentary texts (the precedent text α and the subsequent text β).

"Preservation" of a quotation, in view of the combination of the definition factor and what is excluded, refers to the unchanged combination of a specific factor and a specific exclusion in two or more different commentary texts. That is to say, a is excluded by the same factor x in both α and β.

"Substitution" of a quotation refers to the changed combination of the definition factor and what is excluded between the commentary texts. The main character of substitution is that it paraphrases what is excluded in the form of a synonym. That is to say, where originally a or b are excluded by the factor x in α, c is excluded by x in β, where c covers the meaning of the original a and/or b. Therefore, substitution too can be regarded as a variety of preservation.

"Permutation" of a quotation then refers to the changed combination of the definition factor and what is excluded between the commentary texts. That is to say, while a is excluded by a factor x in α, a is excluded by a different factor y in β.

Finally, implicit quotation again takes the form of the "deletion" of what is excluded in the subsequent text. That is to say, a is excluded by factor x in α, however, a is not mentioned in β.

Let me summarize the main points that have been made in the above.

Preservation—a is excluded by x in α,
a is also excluded by x in β.
Substitution— a or b are excluded by x in α,
but c is excluded by x in β.
Permutation— a is excluded by x in α,
but a is excluded by y in β.
Deletion——a is excluded by x in α,
but a is not mentioned in β.

Let us look closely at the preservation, substitution, permutation, and deletion of quotations between the three commentary texts on the *PDhS*, using Table I.

With regard to the occurrence of preservation, we can point out one case in the commentary texts.[27]

(1) *Vy* (I) 1 → *NK* (I) 2

Let us look at this case. "The relation between a bowl and a fruit of jujube" is excluded by factor (I) in the *Vy*. The relation is also excluded by (I) in the *NK*. Therefore preservation of "the relation between a bowl and a fruit of jujube" can be pointed out between the *Vy* and the *NK*.

In turn, with regard to substitution, we can point out three cases in the three commentaries.[28]

(1) *Vy* (I) 1 → *Kir* (I) 1
(2) *Vy* (II) 2–a, (II) 3–a → *NK* (II) 1
(3) *Vy* (II) 2–a, b, (II) 3–a, b → *Kir* (II) 1

Let us look at case (1) first. "The relation between a bowl and a fruit jujube" is excluded by factor (I) in the *Vy*. The relation is under the relation of conjunction. On the other hand, conjunction itself is explicitly excluded by factor (I) in the *Kir*. Therefore, substitution of "conjunction" for "the relation between a bowl and a fruit jujube" occurs between the *Vy* and the *Kir*.

Regarding case (2), both "the relation of largeness in the ether and the articulated word 'largeness' for largeness in the ether," under the relation of the denoted and the denoter, and "the relation of desire in a soul and consciousness of desire in the soul," under the relation of an object and the cognition of the object, are excluded by factor (II) in the *Vy*. Each relata in these relations exists in the same place, as Figure 2 and Figure 3 indicate. "The relation of merit and pleasure," whose relata also exist in the same place, as Figure 8 indicates, is excluded by factor (II) in the *NK*. Therefore, substitution of "the relation of merit and pleasure" for two relations in the *Vy* can be pointed out between the

27. On the reading of "*Vy* (I) 1" etc., in this chapter, the name of the text is indicated at the beginning, next the number of the factors of the definition is indicated and, last, the number or letter indicates what is excluded by each factor as indicated in table I.
28. Hirano [2010a: 150] refers to three cases of substitution. Among cases, a case "*Vy* (I) 2, (I) 3 → *Kir* (I) 2" is wrong.

Vy and the *NK*.

Let us last look at case (3). The relation of the denoted and the denoter—<a> the relation of largeness (*mahattva*) in the ether and the articulated word "largeness" (*mahattvaśabda*) for largeness in the ether, and <b> the relation of the ether (*ākāśa*) and the articulated word "ether" (*ākāśaśabda*)—is excluded by factor (II) in the *Vy*. Moreover, the relation of an object and the cognition of the object—<a> the relation of desire (*icchā*) in a soul and consciousness of desire (*icchālambanavijñāna*) in the soul, and <b> the relation of a soul (*ātman*) and the cognition of the soul (*ātmālambanajñāna*)—is also excluded by factor (II) in the *Vy*. The *Kir* excludes "the relation of denoted and the denoter etc." by factor (II). When we then consider that "the relation of an object and the cognition of the object" is paired up with "the relation of the denoted and the denoter" in the *Vy*, it may safely be assumed that the word "etc." (*ādi*) in "the relation of the denoted and the denoter etc." in the *Kir* implies "the relation of an object and the cognition of the object." Moreover, although the *Kir* does not provide a specific relation for it, his reasons for exclusion of the relation by factor (II) is that "the relation of denoted and the denoter etc." occurs by accidental attribute. The specific relations provided in the *Vy* could be applied to Udayana's reason. Therefore, substitution of "the relation of the denoted and the denoter etc." for the above four relations in the *Vy* can be pointed out between the *Vy* and the *Kir*.

Regarding permutation, we can again point out three cases in the commentary texts.[29]

(1) *Vy* (I) 2, 3 → *Kir* (II) 1
(2) *Vy* (II) 1 → *NK* (I) 1
(3) *Vy* (II) 2–b → *NK* (IV) 1

Let us look at case (1) first. "The relation of the denoted and the denoter" and "the relation of an object and the cognition of the object" are excluded by factor (I) in the *Vy*. Although the *Vy* does not provide a specific relation for each or them, we have constructed examples such as "the relation of a pot and the articulated word 'pot'" in Figure 6 for the former case, and "the relation of a pot and the cognition for the pot" in Figure 7 for the latter. The *Kir* excludes "the relation of denoted and

29. Hirano [2010a: 151] refers to three cases of permutation. Among cases, a case "*Vy* (III) 2 → *NK* (I) 1" is wrong.

the denoter etc." by factor (II) without providing a specific relation it. As we have already mentioned, it may safely be assumed that the word "etc." (*ādi*) in "the relation of the denoted and the denoter etc." in the *Kir* implies "the relation of an object and the cognition of the object." Udayana's reason for exclusion of the relation by factor (II) is that "the relation of denoted and the denoter etc." occurs by accidental attribute. The constructed specific relations provided in the *Vy* could be covered by Udayana's reason. Therefore, permutation can be pointed out between the *Vy* and the *Kir* with reference to this relation.

Let us look at cases (2) next. "The relation between the ether and a [flying] bird" is excluded by factors (II) in the *Vy*. But the relation is excluded by (I) in the *NK*. Therefore permutation can be pointed out between the *Vy* and the *NK* with reference to this relation.

Let us look at case (3) last. "The relation of the ether and the articulated word 'ether'" is excluded by factor (II) in the *Vy*. The same relation, however, is excluded by factor (IV) in the *NK*, and, therefore, permutation can again be pointed out between the *Vy* and the *NK* with reference to this relation.

Finally, with regard to deletion, we can point out five cases in the three commentaries.[30]

(1) *Vy* (I) 2 → *NK*
(2) *Vy* (I) 3 → *NK*
(3) *Vy* (II) 1 → *Kir*
(4) *Vy* (II) 3–b → *NK*
(5) *Vy* (III) 1 → *NK*, *Kir*

For the moment let us look closely at (5). "The village and the trees" are excluded by factor (III) in the *Vy*. But they are not mentioned in the *NK* and the *Kir*. Therefore, with regard to them, deletion can be pointed out between the *Vy* and these subsequent texts, the *NK* and the *Kir*. Regarding the other 4 cases too, what is excluded by factor, and that which is specifically mentioned in the *Vy*, is not then mentioned later. That is to say, these examples above are deleted in the subsequent texts.

It follows from what has been said that, when we analyze the genesis of commentary texts from the viewpoint of quotation theory, the commentary texts themselves are generated by this quotation. In other words, they are the result of preservation, substitution, permutation,

30. Hirano [2010a: 151] refers to nine cases of deletion. Among cases, 4 cases "*Vy* (II) 2–a → *Kir*," "*Vy* (II) 2-b → *Kir*," "*Vy* (II) 3–a → *Kir*," and "*Vy* (III) 2 → *Kir*" are wrong.

and deletion of already-known information from preceding texts.[31] However, we should not conclude that only the oldest text, in this case the *Vy*, has presented original thought. If it is emphasized that the commentary texts are generated by quotation of already-known information, the same is true of the original. That is to say, we can think of the *Vy*, although it does not have preceding commentary texts on the *PDhS*, as also composed of information drawn from different earlier texts.[32]

The classification of quotation into four forms—preservation, substitution, permutation, and deletion—is based on the way in which information is conveyed. From this viewpoint, let us consider the qualities of the information that is conveyed by each of these four forms of quotation. Preservation takes the form of the unchanged combination of old information. Therefore, information which preservation conveys can be regarded as that information which has been restricted from being re-interpreted and is therefore non-violated. Substitution and permutation take the form of the changed combination of old information. Information which substitution and permutation convey can therefore be regarded as new information, produced via the new combination of old information. Deletion takes the form of old information not perceived in a new commentary text. Since brief and simple explanation was demanded in Indian philosophy, there was a tendency for these commentary texts to omit or delete common and already-known information. Taking this tendency into consideration, information conveyed via deletion can be regarded as common, already-known, and prevalent information, which was probably of no value for making specific reference to.

Furthermore, when comparing the three commentary texts on the *PDhS*, we notice that the amount of commentary on each category decreased over time.[33] If we combine and measure the amount of comments on the definition of inherence in the *PDhS* and compare this to the three commentary texts, the *Vy* is roughly 49 times larger,

---

31. Wada [2010] considers the Navya-nyāya texts through the quotation theory.
32. Our concern here is to consider this relationship between texts, in which a particular text is generated by virtue of quotation from a preceding text. Tracing the specific source of quoted information is not our present concern.
33. We can also point out the decrease in the amount of comments of the three commentary texts in the definition chapter of substance, quality, activity, and particular.

the *NK* is 30 times larger, and the *Kir* is 8.8 times larger than the *PDhS*. An increase of "deletion" between the three commentary texts helps to account for this decrease in the amount of comments on inherence between the three commentary texts.[34] If we view this from a different perspective, we may see that it implies an expansion and communalization of knowledge about inherence in the Vaiśeṣika school within the period from the *Vy* to the later *Kir*.[35]

3.5 The System of Commentary Text from Quotation Theory

(1) Commentary texts are generated by combining information quoted and drawn from precedent texts. When new commentary texts are generated, some preexisting information is preserved, substituted, permuted, and deleted, as we have observed using the three commentary texts on the *PDhS* with reference to the definition of inherence. However, this does not mean that new commentary texts do not convey new and original information. Original information occurs from the combination of old information. In this case, the combination of a definition factor and what is excluded is re-combined in a newer commentary text, showing new and original interpretation of inherence.

(2) When comparing the three commentary texts on the *PDhS*, it is clear that the amount of commentary on the definition of inherence decreases over time. Deletion of information can be regarded as a main cause of this decrease in the amount of commentary between the three commentary texts. We can assume that the deleted information is already-known, prevalent, and common information for the commentators. Therefore, it is often omitted or deleted in the commentary texts on the basis of demand for brief and simple explanations. In other words, we might say that the deleted information is of no value for making reference to, but is instead conveyed orally.

On the other hand, we also have to admit that the commentary texts include information without deleting, even if the information must have been already known, prevalent, and common. Conjunction,

34. We should also consider that "substitution" contributes to the decrease in the amount of comments on inherence between the three commentary texts as well.
35. In Chapter 4 "The Interaction between Text and Context," I will analyze and discuss in detail this decrease in the amount of comments on inherence's definition in the *PDhS* between the three commentary texts.

a relation well known as the antithesis of inherence in the Vaiśeṣika school, is treated as such a kind of information in the commentary texts. The fact that information on conjunction is quoted explicitly in the commentary texts suggests that information on conjunction must have been indispensable to understanding inherence. Therefore, it seems reasonable to say that conjunction was quoted in the form of preservation and substitution in the commentary texts following the *Vy*. Preservation refers to the unchanged combination of information (the definition factor and what is excluded). Although substitution refers to the changed combination of information, it is also a variety of preservation. In other words, this analysis may show that conjunction was not allowed to be re-interpreted, or at least extensively re-interpreted, in the discussion of inherence by the commentators, and, we may then regard preserved or substituted information as non-violated information. In addition, although the concept of "tradition" is ambiguous, one may say that traditional views are represented in information that is conveyed through preservation and substitution.

(3) When we admit that already-known and common information, which is regarded as unworthy of quotation, is deleted in new commentary texts, a new commentary text loses its character as an autonomous text. The "deleted" information cannot be known by reading the new commentary text only, since the new commentary text does not explicitly quote it. Hence, if a reader of the commentary text desires basic information as to inherence, they must refer to not only the new text, but also to the old texts. On the other hand, if the reader refers to the old texts only, they would miss the latest information. Viewed in this light, commentary texts on the same original source material should be regarded as one whole, where complete information is conveyed by the commentary texts group.

(4) Moreover, if we look at deletion from a different perspective, not bound by the texts only, we will expect a group and community, which memorizes and holds "deleted" information in common, denoted by this activity. It is difficult to imagine that the commentary texts were made, not for the public, but for individuals only. Namely, the deleted information must have been well-known and common, not only for the commentator himself, but also for the group and community as a whole. Working within this background, the commentators could actively delete the already-known information in their commentary texts. In turn, this group or community itself, in addition to the commentary

texts, becomes another implement of communication for conveying well-known and common information. That is to say, such a social context as groups and communities also plays an important role in the genesis of the commentary texts. Viewed in this light, we might regard an aspect of the concept of "school" in Indian philosophy as a group or community which memorizes deleted information, in common.

Chapter 4

The Interaction between Text and Context

4.1 Introduction

In Chapter 4, we analyze the genesis of the commentary text in Indian philosophy, taking its context into consideration, in order to reveal the commentary text system in general. It is no doubt that a main function of a commentary text is to comment on an original text.[1] Further, when the commentary texts of an original text are compared, it is certain that the comments in each commentary text are rarely the same. This diversity of comments means that each of the commentary texts surrounding a primary text conveys different contents. In other words, each text contains arguments which emphasize different points.

We consider here the emphatic points of such argument between the three commentary texts: the *Vy* of Vyomaśiva, the *NK* of Śrīdhara, and the *Kir* of Udayana, written in regard to the *PDhS* of Praśastapāda, concentrating, not on the contents themselves but their forms—that is to say, on the amount of comments itself. Of course, we could place our emphasis on the argument of a text, concentrating on its contents, which is a common way of considering a text. However, by paying attention to form, we can discern a particular point of argument that we might not, or, more likely, could not, realize in the traditional way. Even if any doubt remains regarding whether the amount of comments is an indicator of a text's emphasis on information, it cannot be denied that the amount of comments can certainly be regarded as one indication of a text's particular emphasis. We will take this approach as a standard for judging the emphasis on information in the commentary texts on the *PDhS*. We will then specifically analyze each comment on inherence's

1. Regarding the concept of "original text" in this book, see fn. 21 in Chapter 2.

definition in the *PDhS*.

The outline of consideration in this Chapter is as follows: I will show the differences between what each commentary text emphasizes. The emphasis in each commentary text is decided by the proportion of its comments on each factor (part) composing inherence's definition in the *PDhS*. Next, we will consider the influence of the context on each of these points of emphasis, taking the objection of the opponents as an instance of context. Lastly, we will offer a means of considering the genesis of the commentary texts themselves, based on this interaction between text and context within the commentary text, clarifying this system.

4.2 The Synopsis of the Chapter of the Definition of Inherence in the *Vy*

To return to the text at the center of this discussion, the *PDhS*, which, again, is an original text for the commentary texts, the *Vy*, the *NK*, and the *Kir*, considered in this Chapter, defines "inherence" as follows:

> That which is the relation, being a cause of the idea "[this is] here (this is in that)," between entities that fix without being separate [from each other], which [stand as] the superstratum and the substratum, is inherence.
> (*PDhS*, no. 9: *ayutasiddhānām ādhāryādhārabhūtānāṃ yaḥ sambandha ihapratyayahetuḥ sa samavāyaḥ.*)

And as I have discussed at Section 3.1 in Chapter 3, this definition can in turn be separated into four factors:

(I) entities that fix without being separate [from each other] (*ayutasiddha*),
(II) entities that [stand as] the superstratum and the substratum (*ādhāryādhārabhūta*),
(III) the relation (*sambandha*), and
(IV) a cause of the idea "[this is] here" (*ihapratyayahetu*).

Counting these four factors as our standard for the division of the contents of each "chapter of inherence's definition" in the three commentary texts, we can make a synopsis of each chapter in these three commentary texts. That is to say, the content in each commentary text is divided on the basis of which of these four factors each commentary text comments on. Of course, we may take another standard for division. However, the general way in which the commentary texts comment on the definition of inherence is to select a particular factor from the definition and to make, briefly or in detail, some comments on it. Therefore, these four factors may be a better standard for dividing the content. As a consequence of our way for dividing these texts, we will see that the titles of the first sections in the synopsis, shown below, of each commentary text are expressed with one of the four factors.

In turn, when the factors composing the definition of inherence in the *PDhS* are regarded as the standard for division of the comment in the *Vy*, we can divide it into six sections as follows.[2]

[1] The relation (*sambandha*)

[2] Entities that [stand as] the superstratum and the substratum (*ādhāryādhārabhūta*)
  [2.1] The relation between the ether and a [flying] bird
  [2.2] The cognition of "here" for the ether and the relation (*sambandha*)—1
  [2.3] The cognition of "here" for the ether and the relation (*sambandha*)—2

[3] Entities that fix without being separate [from each other] (*ayutasiddha*)

[4] Entities that [stand as] the superstratum and the substratum (*ādhāryādhārabhūta*)
  [4.1] The relation of the denoted and the denoter, and that of an object and the cognition of the object—1
  [4.2] The relation of the denoted and the denoter, and that of an object and the cognition of the object—2

[5] Entities that fix without being separate [from each other] (*ayutasiddha*)
  [5.1] Addition of a restriction (*eva*) to *ayutasiddha*
  [5.2] Pointing out a defect of non-being of inherence

[6] A cause of the idea "[this is] here" (*ihapratyayahetu*)
  [6.1] Presentation of a syllogism for the proof of existence of

2. On the translation of the chapter of inherence's definition in the *Vy*, see Part II.

relation
[6.2] Explanation of the syllogism

4.3 The Synopsis of the Chapter of the Definition of Inherence in the *NK*

When the factors of the definition are regarded as the standard for the division, the comment of the *NK* can be divided into four sections. The synopsis of the *NK* is as follows.[3]

[1] Entities that fix without being separate [from each other] (*ayutasiddha*)
- [1.1] Consideration of separate existence (*yutasiddhi*)
- [1.2] The relation between the eternal entities

[2] Entities that [stand as] the superstratum and the substratum (*ādhāryādhārabhūta*)
- [2.1] The relation of merit and pleasure
- [2.2] The relation between the ether and a [flying] bird

[3] A cause of the idea "[this is] here" (*ihapratyayahetu*)

[4] Entities that fix without being separate [from each other] (*ayutasiddha*)
- [4.1] The relation between a bowl and a fruit of jujube
- [4.2] Objection to the expression *ayutasiddha*
- [4.3] Answer to the objection
- [4.4] Difference between inherence and conjunction

4.4 The Synopsis of the Chapter of the Definition of Inherence in the *Kir*

Finally, the synopsis of the chapter of inherence's definition in the *Kir*, which results in three sections, is as follows.[4]

[1] Entities that fix without being separate [from each other] (*ayutasiddha*)

---

3. On the translation of the chapter of inherence's definition in the *NK*, see Part III.
4. On the translation of the chapter of inherence's definition in the *Kir*, see Part IV.

[1.1] Consideration of *ayutasiddha*
[1.2] The relation of conjunction (*saṃyoga*)

[2] Entities that [stand as] the superstratum and the substratum (*ādhāryādhārabhūta*)

[3] A cause of the idea "[this is] here" (*ihapratyayahetu*)

4.5 The Focus of Commentary in the Three Commentary Texts

Let us then consider the emphasized point in each commentary text, concentrating on form. Specifically, let us look at how much of the comment each commentary text devotes to each factor (part) of the definition of inherence in the *PDhS*.

First of all, when comparing the three commentary texts—the *Vy*, the *NK*, and the *Kir*—there is the immediately recognizable tendency whereby the amount of comments on each category decreases over time.[5] As for the chapter of inherence's definition, when the amount of writing in the *PDhS* is measured in terms of bytes, it results in 98 bytes.[6] When we then compare it to the three commentary texts, the *Vy* is roughly 49 times larger, the *NK* is 30 times larger, and the *Kir* is 8.8 times larger than the original *PDhS*. Based on the above synopses, we can show the number of bytes allotted to a particular comment on each of the four factors and its approximate proportion to the whole text in each commentary text in Table I, where B stands for byte, as follows:

5. For instance, we can point out the decrease in the amount of comments on each definition of substance (*dravya*), quality (*guṇa*), activity (*karman*), and particular (*viśeṣa*) in the three commentary texts.
6. Bytes referred to in this Chapter are measured on the Text Edit, ver. 1.5 (224), in Mac OS 10.5.8.

Table I: The amount of bytes and proportion of comments on each factor in the three commentary texts.

Factor \ Text	the *Vy* (4811 B)	the *NK* (2948 B)	the *Kir* (865 B)
(I)	[3]—288 B—6% [5]—788 B—16% total 22%	[1] 986 B—34% [4]—1427 B—48% total 82%	[1]—447 B—52% total 52%
(II)	[2]—1093 B—23% [4]—1459 B—30% total 53%	[2]—337 B—11% total 11%	[2]—213 B—24% total 24%
(III)	[1]—323 B—7% [2]—129 B—3% total 10%		
(IV)	[6]—731 B—15% total 15%	[3]—198 B—7% total 7%	[3]—205 B—24% total 24%

B=byte (I) entities that fix without being separate [from each other] (*ayutasiddha*), (II) entities that [stand as] the superstratum and the substratum (*ādhāryādhārabhūta*), (III) the relation (*sambandha*), (IV) a cause of the idea "[this is] here" (this is in that) (*ihapratyayahetu*).

I will briefly explain how to read Table I. The number in the square bracket (such as [6]) indicates the section number of the synopsis in the commentary texts. Following the square bracket, the number of bytes of the section in each commentary text is referred to (such as [6]—731 B). Following this, the proportion of the number of bytes on each section to the whole is referred to (731 B—15%). Then, the total percentage of the number of bytes, which each of the commentary texts devotes to commenting on each factor, is referred to (i.e., total 15%). Therefore, regarding the comments of the *Vy* on factor (I)—"the entities that fix without being separate [from each other] (*ayutasiddha*)"—we are able to see from Table I that the *Vy* devotes 288 bytes to section [3] and 788 bytes to section [5]. These bytes occupy 6% and 16%, respectively, of the chapter of inherence's definition in the *Vy*. Further, the total proportion of bytes, which is allotted to commenting on (I) in the chapter of inherence's definition in the *Vy*, is 22%.

For an easier understanding of the data in Table I, we can make use of the following pie charts:

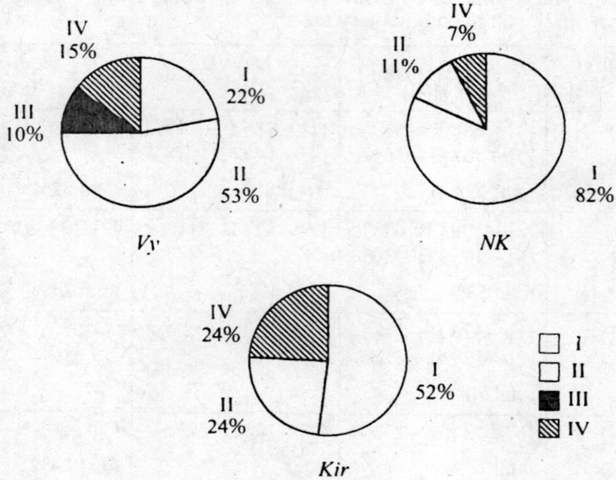

The proportion of comments on factors

As the chart for the *Vy* indicates, the *Vy* devotes more comments to factor (II), the *NK* gives more comments to (I), as does the *Kir*. From the viewpoint that the amount of comments is a standard of indication for the particular informational emphasis of a text, we may say that the information which the *Vy* conveys in the chapter shows an emphasis on (II) among the four factors, and that information which the *NK* and the *Kir* convey emphasizes (I).

Let us now attempt to extend the range of our observation into what information each of the three commentary texts conveys as a whole. The *Vy* comments equally on all factors, although 53% of the whole is devoted to (II). The *NK* devotes a remarkably large amount of comments to (I)—about 82%—without commenting on (III). Lastly, the *Kir* devotes about 52% to (I) without commenting on (III).

On average, considering the proportion of comments on each factor in the three commentary texts, factor (I) is 52%,[7] factor (II) is about 29.33%, factor (III) is about 3.33%, and factor (IV) is

7. The figure 52% is calculated by adding the total proportion of the bytes for (I) in each commentary text and then dividing by three. Other figures are calculated in the same manner.

about 15.33%. That is to say, when we regard the three commentary texts, sharing the same original source material, as one whole, the commentary texts-group devotes the most amount of comments to factor (I).

4.6 A Cause for the Change in Point of Emphasis

We have already clarified an aspect of the system of the commentary text in Indian philosophy, based on communication theory, in Chapter 2. When we take this system into consideration, it is possible to assume that the objections from opponents are a cause for the change of emphasis, which we noted above, in the three commentary texts.

In Chapter 2 I pointed out that a commentary text consists of two types of communication—between the author of the original text and commentators, and between the commentator and his opponents. In the former communication, a commentary text is of a manifestation of the "interpretation" of the original text, and in the latter communication, it is of a manifestation of the "answers" to the counterarguments. Then we concluded that the system of the commentary text is marked by the interaction between the "interpretation" of the original text and "answers" to counterarguments.

I shall outline here, although only briefly, one aspect of this interaction. The original text can be said to only provide fragmentary knowledge or information of the doctrines to the commentator for use in answering objections, since objections themselves often target unresolved or unwritten philosophical issues in the original text. Therefore, the commentator needs to give careful consideration to counterarguments any time he interprets the original text. In other words, the commentator needs to provide an interpretation which resolves the points of the counterargument, and a clear demonstration of the counterargument's invalidity is declared in his "answer." Thus, we can point out the influence of this "answer" to the counterarguments on the commentator's "interpretation." This is one aspect of the interaction noted above in the system of the commentary text itself.

The interaction between interpretation and answers in the system of the commentary text leads to a tendency for more objections against some factors, which in turn causes more comments on that particular factor in the commentary texts. The differences in emphasis between the three commentary texts can be explained by this relationship. That is to say, by, or in, the time of the *Vy*, objections against inherence were mainly directed against factor (II)—"entities that [stand as] the superstratum and the substratum"—and issues concerned with (II). Therefore, the *Vy* allotted more comments to (II). Moreover, in view of the observation that the *Vy* comments equally on all factors, it is possible that the objections that were raised against all factors had remained unanswered until the time of the *Vy*. It is reasonable to suppose that since the *Vy* was the first available commentary text on the *PDhS*, it had to equally address the objections against all factors.

Next, we can assume that objections against inherence mainly related to only factor (I)—"entities that fix without being separate [from each other]"—and issues concerned with (I) by, or in, the time of the *NK*. Therefore, the *NK* allotted more comments to (I). On the other hand, it does not comment on (III)—"the relation"—at all. A hypothesis for this lack of comments on (III) may be that there was no objection against (III) and that, even if there were objections, they might have been not worth answering, or the *Vy* might have given a sufficiently adequate answer for the *NK* not to address them.

Last, we can assume that more objections against inherence were addressed to factor (I) and issues concerned with (I) by, or in, the time of the *Kir* as well. Therefore, the *Kir* allotted more comments to (I). Regarding the lack of comments on (III) in the *Kir*, we might offer the same hypothesis as mentioned above. Moreover, we can observe that the *Kir* gives a relatively large amount of comments on (IV)—"a cause of the idea '[this is] here'"—and that the proportions of the amount of comments to factor (IV) in the three commentary texts increase. There is a possibility that the point of objections had been gradually switched to an epistemological concern.

As we have seen, when the three commentary texts are regarded as one whole,[8] the commentary texts-group allots the most comments to factor (I), whose proportion to the whole is 52%. Factor (I), "entities that fix without being separate [from each other] (*ayutasiddha*)," must have been the key point for opponents seeking to defeat the concept of inherence held by the Vaiśeṣika school. In fact, it seems reasonable to suppose that factor (I) plays an important role in the definition. The

8. Section 3.5 in Chapter 3 argues that the commentary texts on the same original source material should be regarded as one whole, where complete information is conveyed by the commentary texts-group.

three commentary texts agree in interpreting the role of factor (I) as that which distinguishes inherence from conjunction (*saṃyoga*), a relation well known as the antithesis of inherence in the Vaiśeṣika school. We might argue that, if the commentary text could not have provided interpretation and answers in terms of this factor (I), sufficient to match with its doctrine, this would mean, for the school itself, that the difference between important relations—conjunction and inherence—would vanish, and that the structure of the world, which the Vaiśeṣika insisted on, would collapse.

Moreover, the combination of (I) and conjunction itself is not changed in the three commentary texts.[9] This *unchanged* combination results in a steady interpretation of (I) between the commentary texts. When we regard this steady interpretation as an indicator of traditional views which were not allowed to be re-interpreted and, therefore, to be violated, it is no exaggeration to say that since factor (I) had such a relation to the traditional views on inherence in the Vaiśeṣika, it became a target for opponents, so that the commentary texts-group might devote most of their attention to (I).

4.7 The System of Commentary Text from the Contextualism

Each of the commentary texts, the *Vy*, the *NK*, and the *Kir*, emphasizes and focuses on different points when commenting on the definition of inherence in the *PDhS*, although they comment on the same material text. We can see the degree of emphasis employed in each specific text to be different, indicating the proportion of comments therein.

As a possible cause of this change in, and differences in degree of, emphasis between the three commentary texts, the existence of objections from opponents can be expected. Based on the system in which the interaction between the "interpretation" and the "answer" occurs, we can say that more objections against a portion or a complete factor in the definition cause more comments on that portion or factor in the commentary text. Objections are the context for the commentary texts. Therefore, we are now able to see that the commentary text is under the influence of its context. At the same time, we can say that

9. With regard to the significance of the unchanged combination of (I) and conjunction in the three commentary texts from a viewpoint of quotation theory, see sections 3.4 and 3.5 in Chapter 3.

the context is under the influence of the text as well, since enough comments on a portion or factor in the definition lead to measures for preventing opponents from making such objection against that portion. It is noteworthy that while the philosophic commentary text is considered to be dealing with truth, which is beyond context, it is always under the influence of its context.

Moreover, when we set our eyes to the difference of the date of the three commentary texts, we find that these were made within a span of, at most, only 200 years. Due to the limited materials available to Indian studies, it is a difficult task to truly identify the expected objections within a particular text or any philosophers who raised the objections, which then actually influenced each of the three commentary texts during this 200 years. However, it is possible to make an assumption regarding these objections and to construct a variety of objections that arguably influenced each of the three commentary texts, paying attention to the point of emphasis in each text. Our way of considering text in this Chapter enables us to manifest the context which is not written in the text and influences the text.

Chapter 5

Conclusion

In Chapter 5, I will first review the main points of the arguments made in the previous Chapters 2, 3, and 4, clarifying the meaning-system of the commentary text in Classical Indian philosophy based on the arguments of these previous Chapters.

First, with regard to Chapter 2, we revealed a system of the commentary text from the viewpoint of communication theory. After having argued that basic communication consists of four elements—a sender, code, message, and receiver—we applied this framework to the commentary text in Indian philosophy, and, through this application, made it clear that the commentary text consists of two types of communication. The first type is between the author of the original text and a commentator, while the second is between opponents of a text and the commentator. In the former case, the "sender" is the author of the original text, the "message" is the original text itself, the "receiver" is the commentator, and the "codes" are the doctrine of the school, Sanskrit grammar, etc. In the latter case, the sender is the opponent of a text or doctrine, the message is composed of the objections to this doctrine made by the opponent, the receiver is the commentator who must respond to these objections, and the codes are the doctrines of each school, Sanskrit grammar, etc.

In both forms of communication, the commentator assumes the role of the receiver. His understanding of the message (the original text and the objections) then results in the specific form of "interpretation" and "answers" in each act of communication. The point is that these two aspects, "interpretation" and "answers," exist with reciprocal action. That is to say, when the commentator, acting as a receiver, makes an interpretation of the original text, he needs to provide an interpretation which resolved the points of the counterargument, presenting in his answer to this counterargument, a clear demonstration of it's invalidity. In this point, we can see that the "interpretation" of the original text is influenced by the "answer" to the counterargument. In turn, the "interpretation" of the original text also has an influence on the "answer" to the counterargument, since the answer must be made in accordance with the doctrine of the school; and the doctrine, which the commentator assumes to be valid, is declared in his interpretation. At this point, we can see that the "answer" to the counterargument is under the influence of the "interpretation" of the original text. Considering these arguments, we concluded that the commentary text has a system in which the interpretation of the original text, and the answer to the counterargument, interact with one another.

With regard to Chapter 3, we revealed another aspect of the system of the commentary text, considering the genesis of commentary texts from the viewpoint of quotation theory, utilizing the "definition of inherence chapter" in each of the *Vy*, the *NK*, and the *Kir*, and focusing on how already-known information is quoted in these commentary texts on the original *PDhS*. In this case, the already-known information is composed of the "four factors" constituting the definition of inherence in the *PDhS*, as well as "what is excluded." The specific combination of factors in each commentary text, and what is excluded, was then analyzed by the four forms of quotation—namely, preservation, substitution, permutation, and deletion. For example, "the relation between a bowl and a fruit of jujube" is excluded by factor (I) "entities that fix without being separate [from each other]" (*ayutasiddha*) in the *Vy*. This same "relation" is also excluded by (I) in the *NK*. Therefore, "preservation," which refers to the unchanged combination of already-known information in a following commentary text, can be pointed out between the *Vy* and the *NK*. Through similar analyses to the above example, it was made clear that the commentary texts on the *PDhS* are generated by quotation. To be precise, commentary texts are the result of the preservation, substitution, permutation, and deletion of already-known information from a precedent text. Through these arguments I came to the conclusion that the commentary text has a system in which a following commentary text is generated in the form of quotation from a precedent commentary text.

With regard to Chapter 4, we revealed one more aspect of the system of the commentary text, considering the genesis of commentary texts in terms of the influence of context, again utilizing the "definition of inherence chapter" in the *Vy*, the *NK*, and the *Kir*. Although the

Vy, the *NK*, and the *Kir* comment on the same material text—the original *PDhS*—each emphasizes and focuses on different points when commenting on this definition of inherence in the *PDhS*. As a possible cause of this change in, and differences in degree of, emphasis between the three commentary texts, the existence of objections from opponents can be assumed on the basis of the system of the commentary text from a viewpoint of communication theory, as discussed in Chapter 2. According to this system, more objections against a portion or a complete factor in the definition at a particular historical period cause more comments on that portion or factor in a corresponding commentary text. For instance, as to the fact that the *Vy* allotted more comments to factor (II), "entities that [stand as] the superstratum and the substratum," (*ādhāryādhārabhūta*) we assumed that objections against inherence were mainly directed against this factor (II) and issues concerned with (II) in the time of the *Vy*, with such objections acting as the context for the commentary text. Therefore, we may say that the commentary text is under the influence of its context.

At the same time, the context is under the influence of the text as well, since sufficient comments on a portion or factor in the definition lead to measures for preventing opponents from making objections against that portion. Through these arguments I came to the conclusion that the commentary text has a system in which the commentary text is generated under the influence of its context, although the commentary text also has an influence on this context; namely, in which the interaction between text and context occurs.

Now we may reduce each system, separately discussed in each chapter above, to their simplest combined statement: the commentary text in Indian philosophy has the system, in which the interpretation and the answer by the commentator interact with one another, and in which the commentary text is generated in the form of quotation, under the influence of the commentary's context. For the present, it may be useful to look more closely at the relationships between the elements composing the system, especially the relationships of the context to the other elements, in order to understand the important features of this system. For convenience, each element is referred to as the "interaction," the "quotation," and the "context."

First, regarding the relationship of the "context" to the "interaction," the interaction accepts the context as a necessary factor. The interaction consists of the influence of the "answer" to the counterargument on the "interpretation" of the original text, and the influence of the "interpretation" of the original text on the "answer" to the counterargument. The counterargument (objection) is involved in both forms of influence, since the points of an answer are directed to the "counterargument," and the commentator's interpretation should elude the problems which the "counterargument" pointed out. In turn, the counterargument must be the context for a commentary text. Accordingly, we can say that the interaction is under the influence of the context.

Second, regarding the relationship of the "context" to the "quotation," it is possible to see that the difference in degree of the context's influence on the text is shown by the differences in the form of quotation in a commentary text. Various contextual counterarguments do not uniformly influence the text. Some are strong, and others are not. According to the different degrees of contextual influence on the text, already-known information and thought may be manipulated. And the specific utilization of different forms of quotation—preservation, substitution, permutation, and deletion—could then be regarded as the result of the manipulation of already-known information under this contextual influence. That is to say, suppose that some of the counterarguments were particularly strong. In this case already-known information would be manipulated in the form of "substitution" and "permutation" in order to modify the meaning of the already-known information and to redress the points of the counterarguments. Supposing that the counterarguments were too strong to deal with them via modification of the meaning of already-known information, the already-known information could even be omitted in the form of "deletion." On the other hand, if the counterarguments were weak, the already-known information could be offered in the form of "preservation," which refers to the unchanged combination of already-known information in the following commentary text. From this possible view one may say that the difference *in* the form of quotation in the commentary text mirrors the difference in the degree of contextual influence *on* the commentary text.

The fact that already-known information is utilized in the different forms of quotation between the commentary texts proves clearly that the system of the commentary text is open. Although the same information as that of the original text is input in the commentary texts, the output information is not same between texts. In other words, while commenting on the same initial information, each of the commentary texts ultimately conveys different information through various combinations of the already-known information. If the commentary text did not have an open system, there would be no way that each of the commentary texts could output different information. Thus, we may say that, based on quotation theory, the system is not closed but open. It means that the system is not secluded from outside contextual factors. In addition, this idea is supported by a text's acceptance of the context as a necessary factor for the system.[1] Since the system of the commentary text is open, the commentary texts do not convey constant information, or meaning, but instead convey varying information or meaning.

The commentary text in Indian philosophy, as mentioned above, has a system, in which the interpretation and the answer by the commentator interact with one another, and in which the commentary text is generated in the form of quotation, under the influence of the commentary's context. Simultaneously, it follows from what has been said that it is marked by an open nature. Through this system meaning or information is generated in the commentary text.

Finally, I would like to offer one caveat. Since the characteristic of the commentary text is derived from a consideration of the chapter regarding the definition of inherence in the *Vy*, the *NK*, and *Kir* only, it is obvious that there is not enough evidence to definitively conclude whether or not the characteristic of the commentary text explored herein could be applied to the general phenomenon of commentary texts in classical Indian philosophy. This question needs further consideration. However, this exploration offers a compelling hypothesis for the characteristic of the commentary text in classical India.

1. Regarding the context-dependence's point of view, see Recanati [2004].

PART II

AN ANNOTATED TRANSLATION OF THE DEFINITION OF INHERENCE (*SAMAVĀYA*) CHAPTER IN THE *VYOMAVATĪ*

In Part II, I provide an annotated translation of the definition of inherence chapter in the *Vyomavatī* (*Vy*) of Vyomaśiva (ca. 900–960). The *Vy* is a commentary on the *Padārthadharmasaṃgraha* (*PDhS*) by Praśastapāda (ca. 550–600) together with the *Nyāyakandalī* (*NK*) of Śrīdhara (ca. 950–1000), the *Kiraṇāvalī* (*Kir*) of Udayana (ca. 1050–1100) and so on. We have the following printed texts of the *Vy*:

C: *Praśastapādabhāṣyam*, edited with commentaries (up to Dravya) *Sūktī* of Jagadīśa Tarkālaṃkāra, *Setu* of Padmanābha Miśra and *Vyomavatī* of Vyomaśivāchārya (to the end) by M.M.Gopīnath Kavirāj and Panditraj Dhundhirāj Shāstri, Chowkhamba Sanskrit Series 61, Varanasi: Chaukamba Amarabharati Prakashan, 1983.

S: *Vyomavatī of Vyomaśivācārya*, edited with the *Praśastapādabhāṣya* by Gaurinath Sastri, 2 vols., M.M. Śivakumāraśāstri-granthamālā 6, Varanasi: Sampurnanand Sanskrit University, 1983, 1984.

In addition, we have the following manuscript:

Mys: *Manuscript of Vyomavatī* belonging to the University of Mysore Oriental Research Institute, Ms.-No. C-1575.

In this Part, I have edited Vyomaśiva's text, using the above two editions and Manuscript. Of these three, I have used mainly the S edition. The passages from the C edition and Mys are given as variants in the footnotes. When a passage of the C edition or Mys is used, the passage of the S edition is given in variant. Based on the edited Vyomaśiva's text, I make a translation of the "definition of inherence" chapter in the *Vy*. Regarding the editorial problems on the S edition and the C edition, Halbfass [1993 (1992): 246–247] explains it.

Then, the synopsis of the chapter of inherence's definition in the *Vy* is supplied for convenient reference. It was made by myself, in consideration of the contents of the *Vy*, not shown on the Sanskrit text itself. In the translation, words enclosed by square brackets are words which I have supplied. And words enclosed by round brackets are added to clarify the meaning or significance of ambiguous words in the English translation, or are the original Sanskrit word.

Regarding the translation of the chapter of inherence's definition in the *Vy*, while no scholar has yet completely translated the chapter of inherence's definition in the *Vy* into English, V. Varadachari has offered a summary in Potter (ed.) [1995b (1977): 431]. Honda [2009a] has provided a Japanese translation of the whole *Vy*.

The Synopsis of the Chapter of Inherence's Definition in the *Vyomavatī*

[1] The relation (*sambandha*)

[2] Entities that [stand as] the superstratum and the substratum (*ādhāryādhārabhūta*)
- [2.1] The relation between the ether and a [flying] bird
- [2.2] The cognition of "here" for the ether and the relation (*sambandha*)—1
- [2.3] The cognition of "here" for the ether and the relation (*sambandha*)—2

[3] Entities that fix without being separate [from each other] (*ayutasiddha*)

[4] Entities that [stand as] the superstratum and the substratum (*ādhāryādhārabhūta*)
- [4.1] The relation of the denoted and the denoter, and that of an object and the cognition of the object—1
- [4.2] The relation of the denoted and the denoter, and that of an object and the cognition of the object—2

[5] Entities that fix without being separate [from each other] (*ayutasiddha*)
- [5.1] Addition of a restriction (*eva*) to *ayutasiddha*
- [5.2] Pointing out a defect of non-being of inherence

[6] A cause of the idea "[this is] here" (*ihapratyayahetu*)
- [6.1] Presentation of a syllogism for the proof of existence of relation
- [6.2] Explanation of the syllogism

A Translation of the Chapter of Inherence's Definition in the *Vyomavatī*

[1] The relation (*sambandha*)[1]

Well, then with [the expression] such as "between entities that fix without being separate [from each other] (*ayutasiddha*)," [Praśastapāda] makes an assertion with reference to inherence. Inherence is a real existence in an absolute sense on the basis of the same proof as what has been already mentioned.[2]

The definition [of inherence] is described. Since what does not show an intermediate space[3] [between two entities] also causes the

---

1. TEXT: *atha ayutasiddhānām ityādinā samavāye pratijñāṃ karoti. samavāyaḥ paramārthasan pūrvoktād eva sādhanād iti. lakṣaṇam ucyate. ihapratyayahetutvam antarālādarśanasyāpīti sambandhagrahaṇam. tathā hi, dūrād grāmārāmayor antarālam apaśyatām* (1*iha*1) *grāme vṛkṣā iti jñānaṃ dṛṣṭam.*
VARIANTS: Mys. *igraha.*
2. The real existences of quality (*guṇa*: see the *Vy*, vol. I, p. 22,1), activity (*karman*: see the *Vy*, vol. I, p. 23,4–5), universal (*sāmānya*: see the *Vy*, vol. I, p. 23,18), and particular (*viśeṣa*: see the *Vy*, vol. I, p. 24,13) are also insisted on at the beginning of the chapter of each definition with the phrase "on the basis of a proof that has been already mentioned (*pūrvoktād eva sādhanāt* or *pūrvavatsādhanam*)." The proof itself is shown in detail in the chapter on the substance's definition in the *Vy*: "Substances are real existences, because they are objects of valid cognition. Whatever an object of valid cognition is, it is a real existence like knowledge (*vijñāna*). These (substances) are such objects of valid cognition. Therefore, [substances are] real existences." (the *Vy*, vol. I, p. 20,17–19: *dravyāṇi paramārthasantīty abādhyamānajñānaviṣayatvāt. yad yad abādhyamānajñānaviṣayaṃ tattat paramārthasat, yathā vijñānam. tathā abādhyamānajñānaviṣayāṇy amūni, tasmāt paramārthasantīti.*)
3. The word of "*antarāla* (an intermediate space, an interval in space)" is found in the universal chapter in the *PDhS* (no. 368). The word is used in the argument that universals, for instance, cowness (*gotva*), are not indicated in an intermediate space between entities, for instance, between two cows, since the occurrence of conjunction and inherence is not existent in an intermediate space between entities. For the above portion of the *PDhS*, Vyomaśiva

idea "[this is] here," the word of "relation" (*sambandha*) is referred to [in the definition of inherence in the *PDhS*]. To be more explicit, those who do not see an intermediate space between the village and the trees on the grounds that [they view the village and the trees from] a distance have the idea "the trees are in this village."[4]

---

comments on it and shows absence of material substance and ether as examples of "*antarāla*" in the *Vy* (vol. II, p. 283,5–8: *tathā kim idam antarālaṃ nāma yatra sāmānyasyopalambhaprasaṅgaś codyate? yadi mūrttadravyābhāvaḥ? na tatra gotvādisāmānyam, abhāvatvād eva. atha śabdānumeyam atīndriyam ākāśam, antarālāvasthitaṃ vā ghaṭādidravyam, tatrāpi na gotvādeḥ samavāye pramāṇam astīty anupalambho ghaṭata ity alam.*) Śrīdhara interprets "*antarāla*" as ether, space, motionless-air, or absence of material substance in the *NK* (p. 317,16–17: *antarālam iti ākāśaṃ vā digdravyaṃ vā stimitavegamūrttadravyābhāvo vā ... .*)

4. The point of discussion here is that an intermediate space is actually between the trees (the forest) and a village. That is to say, both of them are far from each other, so that there is no relation (*sambandha*) between them. However, when a man sees a village and the trees (the forest) from a distance, he has the idea "the trees are in the village" by virtue of an imaginary relation between them. Supposed that the definition of inherence is referred to as "That which is a cause of the idea '[this is] here' is inherence," inherence would be established between them. To avoid it, Vyomaśiva interprets that the word "relation" is referred to in the *PDhS*. On my understanding on this point, see the *Prameyakamalamārtaṇḍa*, which is the Jaina's text and is written by Prabhācandra (ca. 990–1020, on the date of Prabhācandra, see the foreword of the *Prameyakamalamārtaṇḍa*) In this text, a dispute with the Vaiśeṣika over the definition of inherence in the *PDhS* is mentioned as follows: the word "relation" in inherence's definition in the *PDhS* has a function of preventing a deviation from the concept of inherence by virtue of the relation between the trees and the village, which causes the idea "the trees are in this village," as the *Vy* does. See the *Prameyakamalamārtaṇḍa* (p. 604,14–16): *na cāntarālābhāvena 'iha grāme vṛkṣāḥ' itīhedam pratyayahetunā vyabhicāraḥ, sambandhagrahaṇāt. na cāsau sambandho 'bhāvarūpatvāt.* Moreover, see the *Nyāyabhūṣaṇa* (p. 128,16–18: *tasmād guṇakriyāśraya eva senādibuddhau pratibhāti abhinnapratibhāsas tu tatra bhrānta eva, dūrād bhedasya 'grahaṇāḍ grāme vṛkṣā iti pratibhāsavat.*) and the translation of the *Nyāyabhūṣaṇa* concerned by Yamakami [1999: 207].

[2] Entities that [stand as] the superstratum and the substratum (*ādhāryādhārabhūta*)[5]

[2.1] The relation between the ether and a [flying] bird

Objection: Even so, there is a deviation [from the concept of inherence] by virtue of the relation between the ether and a [flying] bird, because it is a cause of the idea "[this is] here" and a relation. To be more explicit, we have the cognition "[this flying] bird is in the ether."

Reply: [Praśastapāda includes] the expression of "the superstratum and the substratum" [in the definition] in order to exclude it (the relation between the ether and a flying bird). Moreover, the ether is neither the superstratum nor the substratum, because the relation of the lower and the higher (*adharottarabhāva*) is not [found between the ether and the flying bird]. Indeed, when there is the relation of the lower and the higher between the conjunct substances, there is the relation of the superstratum and the substratum in the same places. [For instance,] we can perceive [the relation of the lower and the higher] between a bowl and a fruit of jujube, etc. But it (the relation of the lower and the higher) is absent from the ether, because it (the ether), a pervader (*vyāpaka*), exists, pervading a [flying] bird.[6]

[2.2] The cognition of "here" for the ether and the relation (*sambandha*)—1[7]

Objection: Well, then since the ether is beyond the senses, the cognition

---

5. TEXT: *tathāpy ākāśaśakunisambandhena vyabhicāraḥ. tad ihapratyayahetuḥ sambandhaś ceti.* [(1]*tathā hi*[1)]*. ihākāśe śakunir iti jñānaṃ dṛṣṭam. tadvyavacchedārtham ādhāryādhāragrahaṇam. na cākāśasyādhāratvam*[(2 2)] *ādheyatvaṃ* [(3]*vā*[3)]*. adharottarabhāvasyābhāvāt. yatra hi saṃyogidravyeṣv adharottarabhāvas tatraivādhārādheyabhāvaḥ kuṇḍabadarādāv upalabdhas tadabhāvaś cākāśe. tasya vyāpakatvena śakuniṃ vyāpya sadbhāvāt.*
VARIANTS: (1) C, *tathāpi*; (2) Mys, *śakuneś vā*; (3) C, *ca*; Mys omits.
6. A similar discussion is mentioned in the *Prameyakamalamārtaṇḍa* (p. 604,16–18): *nāpi 'ihākāśe śakuniḥ' iti pratyayahetunā saṃyogenaḥ. 'ādhārādheyabhūtānām' ity ukteḥ. na hy ākāśasya vyāpitvenādhastād eva bhāvo 'sti śakuner uparyapi bhāvāt.*
7. TEXT: *athākāśasyātīndriyatvād iheti jñānaṃ na syāt. tasya hy aparokṣeṣv eva bhāvāt. tad asat. atīndriye 'py ākāśe iheti jñānaṃ kevalaṃ bhrāntam. tasya vyavacchedārtham upapannam ādhāryādhārapadam. iṣṭañ ca bhrāntehajñānāsya vyavacchedārthaṃ sambandhapadam.*

of "[this is] here" [for the ether] would not occur, because it (the cognition of "[this is] here") occurs for perceptible entities only.[8]

Reply: That is not right. Even if [the ether is] beyond the senses, the cognition of "[this is] here" for the ether occurs [although this cognition is] complete illusion.[9] In order to exclude it (the illusionary cognition of "here" for the ether), [Praśastapāda] places the expression of "the superstratum and the substratum" [in the definition].[10] Then the word of "relation" is requested [in the definition] in order to exclude the illusionary cognition of "[this is] here."[11]

[2.3] The cognition of "here" for the ether and the relation (*sambandha*)—2[12]

However, in order to refute the above objection [that the cognition

---

8. Umesha [1987: 174, fn. 67] points out that such a objection is attributed to the Mīmāṃsakas.
9. According to Vyomaśiva's view, the ether is not a perceptible object, see the *Vy*, vol. I, p. 110,3–4: *nanu sarvam etad āśrayāsiddham. ākāśasadbhāve pramāṇābhāvāt. na. pratyakṣeṇānupalambhe 'py anumānena sadbhāvasiddheḥ.* Then a similar discussion is found in the *NK* (p. 59,13–17: *nanv ākāśasya sadbhāve kiṃ pramāṇaṃ pratyakṣam eva viyati patati patattriṇi cakṣur-vyāpāreṇehāyaṃ pakṣī prāpno neheti niyatadeśādhikaraṇā pratītir iti cet tadayuktam arūpasya dravyasya cākṣuṣatvābhāvāt yo 'py ayam adhi-karaṇapratyayas tatra vitatālokamaṇḍalavyatirekeṇa na dravyāntaraṃ prati-bhāti ata ākāśasya sadbhāve pariśeṣānumānam upanyasyañ śabdasya dravyāntaraguṇatvaṃ niṣedhati.*)
10. At the argument in [2.1] in Part II, it is referred that the relation between the ether and a [flying] bird causes the cognition "[this flying] bird is in the ether." For this, an objection in [2.2] in Part II points out that the relation between the ether and a [flying] bird does not cause the cognition "this is here," since the ether is beyond the senses. For the objection, Vyomaśiva insists that the ether and a [flying] bird cause the cognition "this is here," although this cognition is complete illusion. The illusionary cognition of "here" for the ether can be excluded by the words "the superstratum and the substratum," since the words "the superstratum and the substratum" exclude the relation between the ether and a [flying] bird, which causes the cognition "[this flying] bird is in the ether," from the concept of inherence.
11. I understand that the illusionary cognition of "[this is] here," which is excluded by the word "relation," refers to the cognition "the trees are in this village" mentioned at [1] in Part II and not the cognition "[this flying] bird is in the ether," since the cause of cognition "[this flying] bird is in the ether," that is to say, the relation between the ether and a [flying] bird, can not be excluded by the word "relation."
12. TEXT: *anye tv asya codyasya parihārārtham ā samantāt* [1]*kāśata ity*[1] *ākāśam*

of "here" for the ether would not arise, since the ether is beyond the senses], others think that [the word of] ether (*ākāśa*) has a sense that shines (*kāśate*) on all sides (*ā*: or all through), therefore, the rays of light are addressed as the ether in the figurative application (*upacāra*). Then, the cognition "[this flying] bird is in the ether" arises, since they (the rays of light) are perceptible.

Reply: This is not right. The reason [for this] is that although [the ether] is real in the primary sense, [their opinion has] an unwarrantable stretch of rule (*atiprasaṅga*) with reference to an imagination by virtue of the figurative application [for the ether]. And we have already said that even if [the ether is] beyond the senses, the perception of the ether occurs [although the perception is] illusionary. In order to exclude it (the illusionary perception of the ether), [Praśastapāda includes] a qualification [of "entities that stand as the superstratum and the substratum"].[13] Moreover, since [there is] an absence of material substance [or] the ether [between the village and the trees], a relation does not exist [between the village and the trees].[14]

[3] Entities that fix without being separate [from each other] (*ayutasiddha*)[15]

Objection: Even so, when [the definition] is referred to as "That which is the relation, being a cause of the idea "[this is] here," between entities

---

(2*vartata*2) *ity* (3*upacāreṇākāśaṃ raśmayo*3) *'bhidhīyante. te ca* (4*pratyakṣā*4) *ity upapannam* (5*ihākāśe*5) *śakunir iti jñānam iti manyante. tac cāsat, mukhyasadbhāve 'py upacārakalpanāyām atiprasaṅgāt.* (6*uktañ*6) *cātīndriye 'py ākāśe 'parokṣajñānaṃ bhrāntaṃ tadvyavacchedārthaṃ viśeṣaṇam iti. mūrttadravyābhāvena cākāśena sambandhābhāva eveti.*

VARIANTS: (1) C, *kāśanteti*; Mys, *kāśantepy*; (2) Mys, *varttanta*; (3) C, *upacāreṇākāṃkṣā smayo*; Mys, *upacāreṇākāṣaṃ iti śmayo*; (4) S, C, *pratyakṣam*; (5) Mys, *ihākāśa#*; (6) C, *evañ*. # shows the crapmed letters.

13. See the argument in [2.2] in Part II.
14. Honda [2009a: 42] translates this portion in Japanese as "And there must be no relation with the ether which has an absence of material substance." My translation of the portion is based on my understanding mentioned at fn. 3 in Part II.
15. TEXT: *tathā* (1*api*1) *ādhāryādhārabhūtānāṃ yaḥ sambandha ihapratyayahetuḥ* (2*sa*2) *samavāya ity ukte kuṇḍabadarasambandhena vyabhicāras tadartham ayutasiddhānām iti padam. yutasiddhir vakṣyamāṇā sā* (3*vidyate*3) *yeṣāṃ te yutasiddhās tanniṣedhena cāyutasiddhās teṣām iti.*

    VARIANTS: (1) C, *hy*; (2) Mys omits; (3) Mys, *vidyata*.

that [stand as] the superstratum and the substratum, is inherence," there is a deviation [from the concept of inherence] by virtue of the relation between a bowl and a fruit of jujube.[16]

Reply: In order to [exclude] it (the relation between a bowl and a fruit of jujube), [Praśastapāda includes] the expression "between entities that fix without being separate [from each other] (*ayutasiddha*)" [in the definition]. Those in which the separate existence (*yutasiddhi*) that is going to be stated later[17] exists are entities that fix separately.[18] And by denial of them (the entities that fix separately), the entities that fix without being separate [from each other] occur. [Then, inherence subsists] between them (the entities that fix without being separate from each other).

[4] Entities that [stand as] the superstratum and the substratum (*ādhāryādhārabhūta*)

[4.1] The relation of the denoted and the denoter, and that of an object and the cognition of the object—1[19]

Objection: Even so, when [the definition] is referred to as, "That which

---

16. On the relation between a bowl and a fruit of jujube, see Figure 1 in Chapter 3.
17. Tubb and Boose [2007: 228] explain that "*vakṣyamāṇa* may mean 'to be stated by the *mūlakāra*'." My translation of this portion is dependent on their explanation. In fact, Praśastapāda, being the *mūlakāra*, mentions the concept of separate existence (*yutasiddhi*) in chapter of disjunction (*vibhāga*) of the *PDhS* (no. 190–193). Note that there is a possibility that *vakṣyamāṇa* may refer to the commentator's own work, see Tubb and Boose [2007: 230].
18. A similar discussion is mentioned in the *Prameyakamalamārtaṇḍa* (p. 604,18–22): *nāpi 'iha kuṇḍe dadhi' iti pratyayahetunāḥ 'ayutasiddhānām' ity abhidhānāt. na khalu tantupaṭādivad dadhikuṇḍādayo 'yutasiddhāḥ, teṣāṃ yutasiddheḥ sadbhāvāt. yutasiddhiś ca pṛthagāśrayavṛttitvaṃ pṛthaggatimattvaṃ cocyate. na cāsau tantupaṭādiṣv apy asti, tantūn vihāya paṭasyānyatrāvṛtteḥ.*
19. TEXT: *tathāpy ayutasiddhānāṃ yaḥ sambandhaḥ* (1*sa*1) *samavāya ity ukte vyabhicārābhāvaḥ. tan na. vācyavācakabhāvena* (2*viṣayaviṣayibhāvena*2) *ca vyabhicārāt.* (3*tathā hy ākāśamahattvam ākāśe samavetaṃ mahattvaśabdavācyam ity ākāśamahattvatacchabdayor vācyavācakabhāvaḥ sambandho na ca yutasiddhir vibhinnāśrayasamavāyitvābhāvāt.*3) *tathā hy ākāśamahattvam ākāśe samavetaṃ tadvācakaś ca śabdas tatraivety ayutasiddhatvam. evam icchādyālambanaṃ vijñānam ātmani samavetam icchādayaś ca tatraivety ayutasiddhatve saty eṣāṃ viṣayaviṣayibhāva ity anayor vyavacchedārthaṃ ādhāryādhārapadam. na cātrākāśamahattvaśabdas tanmahattvādhāraḥ, nāpīcchādyālambanavijñānaṃ tadādhāram iti.*

is the relation between entities that fix without being separate [from each other] is inherence," is there not a deviation [from the concept of inherence]?[20]

Reply: This is not right, because there is a deviation by virtue of the relation of the denoted and the denoter (*vācyavācakabhāva*), and by virtue of the relation of an object and the cognition of the object (*viṣayaviṣayibhāva*).[21] To be more explicit, since largeness in the ether, which is inherent in the ether, is denoted by the articulated word "largeness," the relation of largeness in the ether and the articulated word ["largeness"] for it (the largeness) has the state of the denoted and the denoter.[22] Moreover, separate existence does not [consist in both largeness in the ether and the articulated word "largeness" for it], since [both of them] are not inherent in different loci [respectively].[23] To be

---

VARIANTS: (1) S, *saḥ*; (2) C, Mys omit; (3) C omits.

20. The argument in [3] in this Part II refers to the inherence's definition which consists of four parts. An objection, however, in [4.1] in Part II refers to the definition which consists of two parts—"relation" and "entities that fix without being separate [from each other]." The intention of objection seems to insist the more brief definition of inherence, since the examples which have been excluded by four parts can be excluded by only two parts. That is to say, "the village and the trees" is exclude by word "relation," and "the relation between the ether and a [flying] bird" and "the relation between a bowl and a fruit of jujube" are excluded by the words "entities that fix without being separate [from each other]." Therefore, objection seems to say that two other parts—"entities that [stand as] the superstratum and the substratum" and "a cause of the idea '[this is] here' "—would be ineffective.
21. With regard to *viṣayaviṣayibhāva*, which is literally translated as the relation of object and object-possessor, it can be translated as the relation of an object and the cognition of the object, see Uno [1996: 96].
22. On the relation of largeness in the ether and the articulated word "largeness" for largeness in the ether, see Figure 2 in Chapter 3.
23. The *Vy* explains the concept of "separate existence" (*yutasiddhi*) at chapter of disjunction (*vibhāga*), mentioning that separate existence is found in eternal and transient entities (substances). With regard to the case of transient entities, it is explained as follows: "as to transient entities, on the other hand, separate existence [in two entities] means that [the two entities] inhere in separate [or] different loci." (*Vy*, vol. II, p. 85.20: *anityānān tu yuteṣu pṛthagbhūteṣv āśrayeṣu samavāyo yutasiddhir iti.*) Both largeness in the ether and the articulated word "largeness" for it do not inhere in separate entities, but in the same enitity (the ether). That is to say, each of them has the state of sharing a locus (the ether) with the other (*sāmānādhikaraṇya*), therefore, separete existence does not occur in both of them. On the concept of *yutasiddhi* and *vibhāga*, see Nozawa [1999].

more explicit, since largeness in the ether is inherent in the ether and the articulated word ["largeness"], which is the denoter for it (largeness in the ether), [is inherent] in that same place (the ether), [both of them] are the entities that fix without being separate [from each other].

Similarly, since consciousness, which has as its object desire etc., is inherent in a soul, and desire etc. are [inherent] in that same place (the soul), those have the relation of an object and the cognition of it (the object),[24] while being the entities that fix without being separate [from each other].[25]

Therefore, in order to exclude both (the relation of the denoted and the denoter, and that of an object and the cognition of the object), [Praśastapāda includes] the expression "the superstratum and the substratum" [in the definition]. Moreover, in this case, the articulated word "largeness" in the ether does not have the largeness of it (the ether) as a substratum. Then, consciousness that has as its object desire etc. does not have these [desire etc.] as a substratum.[26]

---

24. On the realtion of desire in a soul and consciousness of desire in the soul, see Figure 3 in Chapter 3.
25. Desire (*icchā*), cognition (*buddhi*), pleasure (*sukha*), pain (*duḥkha*), hate (*dveṣa*), and effort (*prayatna*), which are qualities of the soul, are grasped by an internal organ, that is to say, mind (*manas*). See the *PDhS* (no. 93): *buddhi-sukhaduḥkhecchādveṣaprayatnās tv antaḥkaraṇagrāhyāḥ*. Moreover, see the *Vy*, vol. II, p. 143,2–4: *buddhisukhaduḥkhecchadveṣaprayatnānāṃ dvayor ātmamanasoḥ sannikarṣād upalabdhiḥ. buddhyādayo hi ātmani samavetās tatsambaddhena manasā gṛhyante*. Consciousness (*vijñāna*) of these qualities exists in the soul too. Therefore, the residence of the object (these qualities: *viṣaya*) and the cognition of these qualities (*viṣayin*) is the same. That is to say, each of them has the state of sharing a locus (soul) with the other (*sāmānādhikaraṇya*).
26. Largeness in the ether and the articulated word "largeness" for its largeness are qualities of the ether. Two qualities, which have the relation of the denoted and the denoter, reside respectively in the ether by the relation of inherence. However, although two qualities are the entities that fix without being separate from each other, the relation between two qualities is not inherence, because they are not the entities that stand as the superstratum and the substratum. Similarly, desire and consciousness of desire are qualities of a soul. Two qualities, which have the relation of an object and the cognition of the object, reside in the soul by the relation of inherence respectively. For the same reason as largeness in the ether and the articulated word "largeness", the relation of desire in a soul and consciousness of desire in the soul is not inherence. Regarding this argument, see Bhattacharya [1994: 20–21].

[4.2] The relation of the denoted and the denoter, and that of an object and the cognition of the object—2[27]

Objection: But even so, there is a deviation by virtue of both of them (the relation of the denoted and the denoter, and that of an object and the cognition of the object). To be more explicit, even though [the definition] is referred to as, "That which is the relation between entities that fix without being separate [from each other], which [stand as] the superstratum and the substratum, is inherence," there is a deviation by virtue of the same two relations: the relation of the denoted and the denoter, and that of an object and the cognition of the object [as we objected against]. To be more explicit, since the ether is named by the articulated word "ether," both of them (the ether and the articulated word, "ether") are the denoted and the denoter, while being the superstratum and the substratum.[28] Moreover, separate existence does not [consist in them]. Similarly, since the cognition of "I," which rests on a soul, exists in the soul, both (the cognition of "I" and the soul) which [stand as] the superstratum and the substratum are an object (a soul) and the cognition of the object (the cognition of "I"), while being entities that fix without being separate [from each other].[29]

Reply: In order to exclude these [two relations from the concept of inherence], a restriction [must be added in the definition]: "That which is the relation between *only* entities that [stand as] the superstratum and the substratum is inherence."[30] Then, since both the relation of

27. TEXT: *nanv evam apy ābhyām eva vyabhicāraḥ. tathā hy ayutasiddhānām ādhāryādhārabhūtānāṃ yaḥ sambandhaḥ* (1*sa*1) *samavāya ity ukte 'pi vācya-vācakabhāvaviṣayaviṣayibhāvābhyām eva vyabhicāraḥ. tathā* (2*hy*2) *ākāśa-śabdenākāśam abhidhīyata ity anayor* (3*ādhāryādhārabhāve*3) *sati vācya-vācakabhāvaḥ, na cāsti yutasiddhiḥ. evam ātmālambanam aham iti jñānam ātmany evety ayutasiddhatve saty ādhāryādhārabhūtayor asti* (4*viṣayaviṣayi-bhāva*4) *iti. tadvyavacchedārtham avadhāraṇam ādhāryādhārabhūtānām eva yaḥ sambandhaḥ sa samavāya iti. vācyavācakaviṣayaviṣayibhāvayoś cādhāryādhārabhūteṣu tadviparīteṣu ca sadbhāva iti vyavacchedaḥ.*
VARIANTS: (1) S. *saḥ*; (2) C. Mys. *ca*; (3) C. *ādhāryādhārayor abhāve*; (4) C. *viṣayaviṣayībhāva*.
28. On the relation of the ether and the articulated word "ether," see Figure 4 in Chapter 3.
29. On the relation of a soul and the cognition of the soul, see Figure 5 in Chapter 3.
30. The relation of the ether and an articulated word "ether," under the relation of the denoted and the denoter, is excluded by the expression—a cause that the

the denoted and the denoter, and that of an object and the cognition of the object occur in entities that [stand as] the superstratum and the substratum,[31] as well as in the reversed case,[32] [both of the relations] are excluded [from the concept of inherence].[33]

---

idea "[this is] here"—in the *NK*. The reason is that the relation of the denoted and the denoter does not cause the idea "this is here." On this, see B. Shastri [1993: 123], Bhattacharya [1994: 21–22], and [3] in Part III of this book.

31. The case where signifies entities that stand as the superstratum and the substratum is pointed out between the ether and the articulated word, "ether," and between a soul and the cognition of the soul. See Figure 4 and Figure 5 in Chapter 3.
32. The reversed case, which signifies entities that do not stand as the superstratum and the substratum, is pointed out between largeness in the ether and the articulated word "largeness" in the ether, and between desire in a soul and conciousness of desire in the soul. See [4.1] in this Part II.
33. We can point out the narrow application (*avyāpti*) of the definition of inherence. That is to say, although the relation of the ether and the articulated word "ether," and that of a soul and the cognition of the soul are inherence, both relations are excluded by the qualification with a restriction—*only* entities that [stand as] the superstratum and the substratum—in the *Vy*. However, even though the definition has the defect of narrow application, it could be regarded as a correct definition in Indian philosophy. See Sato [1995: 25–27]. Then, a discussion similar to the *Vy* is mentioned in the *Prameyakamalamārtaṇḍa* (pp. 604,23–605,10): *tathāpi 'ihākāśe vācye vācaka ākāśaśabdaḥ 'iti vācyavācakabhāvena 'ihātmani jñānam 'iti viṣayaviṣayibhāvena vā vyabhicāro 'trāyutasiddher ādhārādheyabhāvasya ca bhāvāt; ity apy asāmpratam; ubhayatrāvadhāraṇāśrayaṇāt. etayoś ca yutasiddheṣv apy anādhārādheyabhūteṣv api ca bhāvāt, ghaṭatacchabdajñānavat. nanv evam 'ayutasiddhānām eva' ity avadhāraṇe 'py avyabhicārāt 'ādhārādheya-bhūtānām' iti vacanam anarthakam, 'ādhārādheyabhūtānām eva' ity avadhāraṇe 'ayutasiddhānām' iti vacanavat, tābhyām avyabhicārāt; ity apy asāram; ekadravyasamavāyinām rūparasādīnām ayutasiddānām eva paras-paraṃ samavāyābhāvāt ekārthasamavāyasambandhavyabhicāranivṛttyartham uttarāvadhāraṇam. na hy ayaṃ vācyavācakabhāvādivad yutasiddhānām api sambhavati. tathottarāvadhāraṇe saty api ādhārādheyabhāvena saṃ-yogaviśeṣeṇa sarvadā 'nādhārādheyabhūtānām asambhavatā vyabhicāro mā bhūd ity evaṃ arthaṃ pūrvāvadhāraṇam.* Taking fns. 4, 6, 18 and the above mentioned into consideration, we can see that the Vaiśeṣika view with reference to inherence's definition of the *PDhS*, which is mentioned in the *Prameyakamalamārtaṇḍa*, is similar to the *Vy*'s view. If the date of authors of the *Vy* and the *Prameyakamalamārtaṇḍa* is regarded as ca. 900–960 and ca. 990–1020 respectively in accordance with the previous study, we may say that the Vaiśeṣika view with reference to inherence's definition of the *PDhS*, which the *Prameyakamalamārtaṇḍa* mentions, is based on the *Vy*'s view.

[5] Entities that fix without being separate [from each other] (*ayutasiddha*)

[5.1] Addition of a restriction (*eva*) to *ayutasiddha*[34]

Objection: But if it were so, [the expression] "entities that fix without being separate [from each other] (*ayutasiddha*)" must be useless [for excluding the relation of the denoted and the denoter, and that of an object and the cognition of the object].

Reply: No (this is not right), because this [expression "entities that fix without being separate from each other"], which possesses a restriction, is also another definition. To be more explicit, [it is interpreted as follows:] "That which is the relation between *only* entities that fix without being separate [from each other] is inherence." However, the relation of the denoted and the denoter, and that of an object and the cognition of the object [subsist] between entities that fix separately[35] and that fix without being separate [from each other].[36]

[5.2] Pointing out a defect of non-being of inherence[37]

On this point others mention a defect (fault) of non-being [of

34. TEXT: *nanv evam ayutasiddhānām iti vyartham eva. na. asyāpi sāvadhāraṇasya* (1*lakṣaṇāntaratvāt*1). *tathā hy ayutasiddhānām* (2*eva*2) *yaḥ sambandhaḥ sa samavāya iti. vācyavācakaviṣayaviṣayibhāvau tu yutasiddhānām* (3*ayutasiddhānāñ*3) *ceti.*
 VARIANTS: (1) Mys, *lakṣaṇāṃtaratvāt*; (2) C, *iva*; (3) C, Mys, *ayutasiddhānāṃ*.
35. Although the *Vy* does not provide specific examples for both relations between entities that fix separately, we can construct examples. The relation of a pot and the articulated word "pot," under the relation of the denoted and the denoter, and the relation of a pot and the cognition of the pot, under the relation of an object and the cognition of the object. On the examples, see the *Prameyakamalamārtaṇḍa* (p. 605,1): *ghaṭatacchabdajñānavat* and Figure 6 and Figure 7 in Chapter 3.
36. For instance, there are the relation of the ether and the articulated word "ether" and that of a soul and the cognition of the soul, under the relation of the denoted and the denoter. On both relations, see Figure 4 and Figure 5 in Chapter 3. And there are the relation of largeness in the ether and the articulated word "largeness" for it (the largeness) in the ether and that of desire in a soul and consciousness of desire in the soul, under the relation of an object and the cognition of the object. On both relations, see Figure 2 and Figure 3 in Chapter 3.
37. TEXT: *atra kecid asaddūṣaṇam udbhāvayanti. samavāyāsiddhau yuteṣv*

inherence]. The reason why [a defect (fault) of non-being is pointed out] is that when [the being of] inherence has not yet been proven, separate existence [in two entities] is not [defined as two entities] *inhering* in separate loci [respectively].[38] [That is to say] those in which it (separate existence) exists are not the entities that fix separately. And when an absence of entities that fix without being separate [from each other] occurs by negation of those [which are not entities that fix separately], it comes to the absence of inherence. Then, this is a defect (fault) of non-being, since the definition distinguishes a being. Indeed, if non-being is caused by a definition, this would amount to a fault.

The reason why the definition, "entities that fix without being separate [from each other] (*ayutasiddha*)," does not cause inherence is that there is an absence of the definition, [that is to say, it has already been pointed out that] the absence of entities that fix without being separate [from each other] occurs by virtue of the deny of entities that fix separately.

Reply: Then, this is not right, because the definition [has a function of] making known [the defined property].

[6] A cause of the idea "[this is] here" (*ihapratyayahetu*)

[6.1] Presentation of a syllogism for the proof of existence of relation[39]

Objection: Well, then when the definition is completed by two parts—

āśrayeṣu samavāyo na yutasiddhiḥ. sā vidyate (1*yeṣāṃ*1) (2*te na*2) *yutasiddhāḥ. tatpratiṣedhena cāyutasiddhānām abhāve na samavāya iti. etac cāsaddūṣaṇam, lakṣaṇasya* (3*vidyamānavyavacchedakatvāt*3). *yadi hy avidyamānaṃ lakṣaṇenotpādyeta bhaved etad dūṣaṇam. ayutasiddhānām iti lakṣaṇena* (4*samavāyākaraṇe*4) *yutasiddhānām* (5*abhāvenāyutasiddhānām*5) *abhāva iti* (6*lakṣaṇāsambhava*6) *iti. na caitat, lakṣaṇasya jñāpakatvād iti.*

VARIANTS: (1) C, Mys, *caiṣām*; (2) C, *tena*, Mys, te tena; (3) C, *vidyamānavyavacchekatvāt*; (4) C, *samavāyakaraṇe*; (5) C, *abhāve nāyutasiddhānām*; (6) C, *lakṣaṇasambhava*.

38. See fn. 23 in Part II. The *PDhS* (no. 190) explains *yutasiddhi* as *anityānāṃ tu yuteṣv āśrayeṣu samavāyo yutasiddhir iti.*

39. TEXT: (1*athāyutasiddhānām*1) *evādhāryādhārabhūtānām eva yaḥ sambandhaḥ sa samavāya iti lakṣaṇadvayaparisamāptāv* (2*ihapratyayahetur iti*2) *vyartham, na. parīkṣārthatvāt. tathā hi,* (3*iha tantuṣu*3) *paṭa ityādi ihapratyayaḥ sambandhakāryaḥ, abādhyamānehapratyayatvāt, yo yo 'bādhyamānehapratyayaḥ* (4*sa sa*4) *sambandhakāryaḥ, yatheha kuṇḍe dadhīti* (5*pratyayaḥ*5),

That which is the relation between only entities that fix without being separate [from each other], which [stand as] the superstratum and the substratum, [is inherence], [the word,] "being a cause of the idea '[this is] here.'" would be of no utility.

Reply: No (this is not right), since [the expression "being a cause of the idea 'this is here'"] has a utility of examining[40] [the existence of inherence with the help of means of getting valid cognition (*pramāṇa*s)].[41] To be more explicit,

[Statement of the thesis (*pratijñā*):] The idea "[this is] here," such as "cloth is in its threads" at the beginning, is caused by a relation,

[Statement of the reason (*hetu*):] because [it possesses] the property of being an unsublated idea "[this is] here."

[Exemplification (*udāharaṇa*):] Whatever unsublated idea "[this is] here" is caused by a relation. For example, there is the idea "the coagulated milk is in the pot."

[Application (*upanaya*):] And this (the idea "[this is] here." such as "cloth is in its threads" at the beginning) is also an unsublated idea "[this is] here."

[Conclusion (*nigamana*):] Therefore, it is caused by a relation.

[6.2] Explanation of the syllogism[42]

Objection: Then, in this [syllogism], it is not demonstrated that [the

---

tathā cāyam abādhyamānehapratyayaḥ. (6*sa tasmāt*6) *sambandhakārya iti.*
VARIANTS: (1) C. *tathāyutasiddhānām*; (2) C. *ihapratyayahetuti*; (3) S. C. *tantuṣu*; (4) C, *sa*; Mys omits; (5) C, *juhuyāt*; Mys, *iha yas*; (6) S, C, *tasmāt*.

40. On the concept of examination (*parīkṣā*) in the style of philosophizing which appears in the philosophical texts in India, see Matilal [1990 (1985): 177–178], Halbfass [1993 (1992): 72, 83, n. 8], and Uno [1996: 28]. Although we have no definite information on the concept of examination in the *Vy*, the *Nyāyabhāṣya* (p. 84.2) defines it as follows: examination [means] to ascertain whether the defined property conforms to the definitions with the help of means of getting valid of cognition (*lakṣitasya yathālakṣaṇam upapadyate na veti pramāṇair avadhāraṇaṃ parīkṣā.*) Then, the *NK* (p. 26,24) defines it as follows: examination [means] to consider the defined property in accordance with the definition (*lakṣitasya yathālakṣaṇaṃ vicāraḥ parīkṣā.*)

41. The *Vy* (vol. II, p. 290,26) says that "[the existence of] inherence is inferred on the basis of the idea '[this is] here'" (*ihabuddhyanumeyaḥ samavāyo ...*).

42. TEXT: *na cātra samavāyapūrvakatvaṃ sādhyate, dṛṣṭāntasya sādhyavikalatāprasaṅgāt. nāpi saṃyogapūrvakatvam. kiṃ tarhi.* (1*sambandhamātrakāryatvam*1). *sa ca* (2*saṃyogādivilakṣaṇatvāt*2) *samavāya eveti vakṣyāmas tatparīkṣāyām ity alam* (3*ativistareṇa*3).

idea "this is here"] is based on inherence, since the deficiency of a probandum (inherence) takes place in the example [which is shown in the exemplification]. Moreover, it is not [demonstrated that the idea "this is here"] is based on conjunction. What [is the cause of idea "this is here"] in this case?

Reply: [The idea "this is here"] is caused by the whole class of relations. Then, we will explain in its [inherence's] examination [chapter][43] that [the word of] "that (*sa*)," [in inherence's definition of the *PDhS*, indicates] inherence exactly, since [the indicated relation] is different from conjunction[44] and so on. Therefore, [the consideration of inherence here is] enough, [since we have already explain inherence] at length.

VARIANTS: (1) C, *sambadhamātrakāryatvam*; (2) Mys, *saṃyogādi-vilakṣaṇatvā*; (3) Mys, *ativistāreṇa*.

43. See the *Vy*, vol. II, pp. 289–291.

44. Regarding the argument of conjunction in the *Vy*, see Ramanujam [1979: 93–99].

PART III

AN ANNOTATED TRANSLATION OF THE DEFINITION OF INHERENCE (*SAMAVĀYA*) CHAPTER IN THE *NYĀYAKANDALĪ*

In Part III, I provide an annotated translation of the definition of inherence chapter in the *Nyāyakandalī* (*NK*) of Śrīdhara (ca. 950–1000). The *NK* is a commentary on the *PDhS* together with the *Vy*, the *Kir*, and so on. Then I have edited the "chapter of the definition of inherence" in the *NK*, using the following printed texts of the *NK*:

O: *Nyāyakandalī being a Commentary on Praśastapādabhāṣya, with Three Sub-commentaries*, edited by J.S. Jetly and Vasant G. Parikh, Gaekwad's Oriental Series 174, Vadodara: Oriental Institute, 1991.

R: *Praśastapādabhāṣya (Padārthadharmasaṃgraha) with Commentary Nyāyakandalī by Śrīdhara Bhatta*, edited with Hindi Translation by Durgādhara Jhā, Gaṅgānātha Jhā Granthamālā vol. 1, Varanasi: Research Institute, Sampurnanand Sanskrit Vishvavidyalaya, 1977.

S: *The Praśastapāda Bhāshya with Commentary Nyāyakandalī of Śrīdhara*, edited by Vindhyesvari Prasad Dvivedin, Sri Garib Dass Oriental Series 13, Delhi: Sri Satguru Publications, 1984.

Of these three, I have used mainly the S edition. The passages from the other editions are given as variants in the footnotes. When a passage of another edition is used, the passage of the S edition is given in variant. Based on the edited Śrīdhara's text, I make a translation of the "definition of inherence" chapter in the *NK*. In translating it, I have consulted three commentaries: the *Ṭippaṇa* of Naracandrasūri, the *Pañjikā* of Rājaśekhara Sūri Maladhārī, and the *Nyāyakusumodgama* of Śiḍila Vommideva. These commentaries are in the O edition of the *NK*. According to Potter [1995a (1970)], Naracandrasūri flourished around 1210, and Rājaśekhara Sūri Maladhārī flourished around 1350. He does not mention Śiḍila Vommideva.[1]

Moreover, the synopsis of the chapter of inherence's definition in the *NK* is supplied for convenient reference. It was made by myself, in consideration of the contents of the *NK*, not shown on the Sanskrit text itself. In the translation, words enclosed by square brackets are words which I have supplied. And words enclosed by round brackets are added to clarify the meaning or significance of ambiguous words in the

1. On the three commentary texts on the *NK*, see the introduction in the *Nyāyakandalī* (O) and Thakur [2003: 277-280]. Neither mentions the dates of Śiḍila Vommideva.

English translation, or are the original Sanskrit word. We already have translation inherence's definition in the *NK* in English and Japanese by Jhā [1982 (1915): 32–35] and Honda [1990: 26–28] respectively, both which present complete translation of the *NK*. However, the present translation in Part III would be useful in point of showing the analysis by synopsis and the translation consulted the commentary texts on the *NK*.

The Synopsis of the Chapter of Inherence's Definition in the *Nyāyakandalī*

[1] Entities that fix without being separate [from each other] (*ayutasiddha*)
  [1.1] Consideration of separate existence (*yutasiddhi*)
  [1.2] The relation between the eternal entities

[2] Entities that [stand as] the superstratum and the substratum (*ādhāryādhārabhūta*)
  [2.1] The relation of merit and pleasure
  [2.2] The relation between the ether and a [flying] bird

[3] A cause of the idea "[this is] here" (*ihapratyayahetu*)

[4] Entities that fix without being separate [from each other] (*ayutasiddha*)
  [4.1] The relation between a bowl and a fruit of jujube
  [4.2] Objection to the expression *ayutasiddha*
  [4.3] Answer to the objection
  [4.4] Difference between inherence and conjunction

A Translation of the Chapter of Inherence's Definition in the *Nyāyakandalī*

[1] Entities that fix without being separate [from each other] (*ayutasiddha*)

[1.1] Consideration of separate existence (*yutasiddhi*)[2]

[Praśastapāda] considers the nature of inherence with [the expression] "between entities that fix without being separate [from each other] (*ayutasiddha*)." Separate existence (*yutasiddhi*) [means] different existence, different residence [in space], [or] the state, possessed by both of two relata, of residing in different loci apart from each other.[3] It (separate existence) is not present between two entities that fix without being separate [from each other]. The relation between those [two entities] is inherence. For instance, [there is inherence] between the

---

2. TEXT: *(1samavāyasya svarūpaṃ1) nirūpayati. ayutasiddhānām iti. yutasiddhiḥ pṛthaksiddhiḥ pṛthagavasthitir ubhayor api sambandhinoḥ parasparaparihāreṇa pṛthagāśrayāśrayitvaṃ. sā yayor nāsti tāv ayutasiddhau, tayoḥ sambandhaḥ samavāyaḥ yathā tantupaṭayoḥ. yady api tantavaḥ (2paṭavyatiriktāśraye2) samavayanti, tathāpy ubhayoḥ parasparaparihāreṇa pṛthagāśrayāśrayitvaṃ nāsti, paṭasya tantuṣv evāśrayitvāt. yatra tu dvayor api sambandhinoḥ parasparaparihāreṇa vyatiriktāśrayāśrayitvaṃ tatra yutasiddhiḥ yathā tvagindriyaśarīrayoḥ. śarīraṃ hi tvagindriyaparihāreṇa pṛthagāśraye svāvayave samāśritaṃ, (3tvagindriyaṃ ca śarīraparihāreṇa pṛthagāśraye svāvayave samāśritam,3) tenānayoḥ saṃyogo na samavāyaḥ.*
VARIANTS: (1) R, S, *samavāyasvarūpaṃ*; (2) O, *paṭavyatiriktāḥ paṭe na*; (3) R, S omit.
3. In the chapter of fire (*tejas*) in the *NK* as well, separate existence is explained in reference to the argument of parts (*avayavas*) and whole (*avayavin*). See the *NK*, p. 42,4–6: *pṛthagāśrayāśrayitvaṃ yutasiddhiḥ … pṛthagāśrayāśrayitvaṃ cāvayavāyavinor bhinnatve 'pi nāstīti …* . (Separate existence [means] the state [possessed by the relata] of residing in different loci […]. And although [the whole and its parts] are distinct, there is not the state of residing in different loci between the whole and its parts […].)

threads and the cloth. Even if the threads inhere in a locus other than the cloth (i.e. in the fibers of cotton, *aṃśus*), still both [the threads and the cloth] do not reside in different loci apart from each other, since the cloth resides in the threads only.[4] On the other hand, where both of two relata reside in different loci apart from each other, there is a separate existence [between the two relata]: for instance, between the sense of touch (*tvagindriya*) and the body (*śarīra*). Indeed, the body dwells in the different locus, it's own parts, apart from the sense of touch. And the sense of touch dwells in the different locus, it's own parts, apart from the body.[5] Accordingly conjunction (*saṃyoga*) is between the two

---

4. According to the *Ṭippaṇa*, we can understand that both of two relata, the cloth and its component threads, have the state of residing in different loci (*pṛthagāśrayāśrayitva*) which is one condition of separate existence (*yutasiddhi*), since the threads reside in the cotton fiber and the cloth resides in the threads. However, the cloth does not satisfy another condition, "apart from each other" (*parasparaparihārena*) since the locus of the cloth is the threads as the other relatum. Accordingly, separate existence is not found between the two relata: the cloth and its component threads. See the *Ṭippaṇa* (pp. 47,14–48,9): *tantupaṭayor hi pṛthagāśrayāśrayitvam asti tantūnāṃ svāvayavasamavetatvāt paṭasya tu tantusamavetatvāt paraṃ parasparaparihāro nāsti paṭasya tantuṣv eva samavetatvāt.*
5. According to the Vaiśeṣika, the sense of touch (*tvagindriya*) is not a part (*avayava*) of the body (*śarīra*). The *NK* (p. 161,4–5) refers to a part where the body inheres in as follows: "*... śarīrasya haste samavetatvāt.*" ([...] since the body is inherent in [its] hand.) Then, the *NK* (p. 38,11–13) says "*na ca pañcabhūtasamavāyikāraṇatve śarīrasyaikatvaṃ prāpnoti svabhāvabhedena bhedopapatteḥ. mānuṣaṃ śarīraṃ pṛthivyātmakaṃ gandhavattvāt paramāṇulakṣaṇapṛthivīvat ....*" (And if [the body] had the five elements for [its] inherent cause, the body could not be one only. The reason [for this] is that the diversity [of the body as the effect] is caused by the diversity of natural constitutions [composed of the five elements as the cause]. [We conclude that] the human body is composed of the earth (*pṛthivī*) since [the human body] has smell. Just like the earth in the form of atom.) See Faddegon [1969 (1918): 369] and Miyamoto [1996: 152–159]. With regard to the sense of touch, the *PDhS* (no. 53) says "*indriyaṃ sarvaprāṇināṃ sparśopalambhakaṃ pṛthivyādyanabhibhūtair vāyvavayavair ārabdhaṃ sarvaśarīravyāpi tvagindriyam.*" (The sense of organ [which is one of four products of air] causes all living beings to feel touch, is composed of the parts of air, which are not predominated by the earth etc., and is the sense of touch which is pervading all over the body.) The *NK* (p. 45,17–22) has the same contents as the *PDhS*: "*yat sarvaprāṇināṃ sparśopalambhakam indriyaṃ tat .... vāyvavayavair ārabdham ... tvagindriyam iti samākhyā ....*" To sum up, the *NK* states that the body is composed of the earth and that the sense of touch is composed of the air (*vāyu*). Therefore, the body inheres in the parts—for

[of the sense of touch and the body], inherence is not [between them].[6]

[1.2] The relation between the eternal entities[7]

On the other hand, as to the eternal entities, separate existence [means] different residence [in space, or] the capability of different locomotion (*pṛthaggamanayogyatā*).[8] It (separate existence) is not present between the two entities that fix without being separate [from each other]. That

---

instance, the hands of the body—which are composed of the earth atoms, whereas the sense of touch inheres in the parts which are composed of the air atoms. Moreover, to abide by the doctrine that a whole (*avayavin*) is one in nature, it is necessary that both of the whole and its parts belong to the same class: earthness (*pṛthivītva*), waterness (*āptva*), fireness (*tejastva*), or airness (*vāyutva*). The sense of touch belongs to airness and the body belongs to earthness, so that the sense of touch is not a part of the body. It is just conjunct with the body. See Bhaduri [1975 (1947): 78–81] and the *PDhS*, no. 192: *tvagindriyaśarīrayoḥ pṛthaggatimattvaṃ nāsti yuteṣv āśrayeṣu samavāyo 'stīti parasпareṇa saṃyogaḥ siddhaḥ.*

6. Regarding the argument in this [1.1], see B. Shastri [1993: 117–120] and Bhattacharya [1994: 19].
7. TEXT: *nityānāṃ tu yutasiddhiḥ pṛthagavasthitiḥ pṛthaggamanayogyatā sā yayor nāsti tāv ayutasiddhau. tayor yaḥ sambandhaḥ sa samavāyo yathākāśadravyatvayor iti.*
8. As for "the capability of different locomotion," the *NK* (p. 160,7–9) defines and exemplifies it in the chapter of disjunction (*vibhāga*) as follows: "*dvayor ekasya vā parasparasaṃyogavibhāgahetubhūtakarmasamavāyayogyatā yutasiddhiḥ. dvayoḥ paramāṇvoḥ pṛthaggamanam ākāśaparamāṇvoś cānyatarasya pṛthaggamanam iyaṃ tu nityānām.*" (Separate existence [means] that two [eternal entities] or one [of them] have the capability of having inherence of activity which consists of the cause of conjunction with, and disjunction from, the other. As for two atoms, there is a [mutually] independent locomotion; and as to the ether and the atom, there is a different locomotion on one (atom) of the two. However, this [kind of separate existence] is in the eternal entities.) On the eternal ubiquitous entities, for instance the ether and the space (*diś*), the *NK* (pp. 160,27–161,1) says "*vibhūnāṃ tu dvayor anyatarasya vā pṛthaggamanābhāvān na paraspareṇa saṃyogo nāpi vibhāgaḥ* … ." (However, as to the ubiquitous entities, there is neither mutual conjunction [with the other] nor mutual disjunction [from the other], since there is no different locomotion in one or two [of the ubiquitous entities …].) In this connection, locomotion (*gamana*) is a kind of activity (*karman*) which is of five kinds: throwing upwards, throwing downwards, contraction, expansion, and locomotion. See the *PDhS*, no. 6: *utkṣepaṇāpakṣepaṇākuñcanaprasāraṇagamanāni pañcaiva karmāṇi*. Moreover, the *PDhS* (no. 329) explains "locomotion" as follows: "That which causes conjunction with and disjunction from a place in unfixed direction is locomotion." (*yad aniyatadikpradeśasaṃyogavibhāgakāraṇaṃ tad gamanam iti.*)

which is a relation between such two entities is inherence. For instance, [there is inherence] between the ether (*ākāśa*) and substanceness (*dravyatva*).[9]

[2] Entities that [stand as] the superstratum and the substratum (*ādhāryādhārabhūta*)

[2.1] The relation of merit and pleasure[10]

When [inherence] is defined as, "the relation between entities that fix without being separate [from each other]," that which is the relation of merit (*dharma*) and pleasure (*sukha*), which has a character of the relationship of cause and effect,[11] would also come to be inherence since there is no separate existence between those two [merit and pleasure] that are residing in the same soul.[12] Therefore, [in order to exclude the relation of merit and pleasure from the concept of

---

9. Both the ether and universal do not have locomotion, since activity inheres in the material substances (*mūrtadravyavṛttitva*) only. See the *PDhS* (no. 324). On the concept of "material substances," the *NK* (p. 290,19–20) comments that "inherence in the material substances [means] inhering in the substances that have the delimited magnitude." (*mūrtadravyavṛttitvam avacchinnaparimāṇadravyavṛttitvam.*) In addition, the ether has ultimate dimension (*paramamahattva*). See the *PDhS*, no. 19: *ākāśakāladigātmanāṃ sarvagatatvaṃ paramamahattvaṃ sarvasaṃyogisamānadeśatvaṃ ca*. On the concept of "ultimate dimension," the *NK* (p. 22,15–16) comments that "ultimate dimension [means] having unlimited magnitude." (*paramamahattvam iyattānavacchinnaparimāṇayogitvam.*) Regarding the argument in [1.2], see B. Shastri [1993: 119].
10. TEXT: *ayutasiddhayoḥ sambandha ity ucyamāne, dharmasya sukhasya ca yaḥ kāryakāraṇabhāvalakṣaṇaḥ sambandhaḥ so 'pi samavāyaḥ prāpnoti, tayor ātmaikāśritayor yutasiddhyabhāvāt. tadartham ādhāryādhārabhūtānām iti padam*.
11. On the relationship of cause and effect between merit and pleasure, see the *NK*, p. 260,3–4: ... *dharmādyapekṣād yad utpadyate tat sukham*. (That which is produced on the basis of [...] merit and so on is pleasure.)
12. As defined in [1.1] in Part III, separate existence (*yutasiddhi*) means the state, possessed by both of two relata, of residing in different loci apart from each other. There is no separate existence between merit and pleasure, since both of them do not reside in different loci. That is to say, since each of merit and pleasure has the state of sharing a locus (soul) with the other (*sāmānādhikaraṇya*), their loci are not different but the same. On the relation of merit and pleasure, see Figure 8 in Chapter 3.

inherence, Praśastapāda includes in the definition] the expression, "between entities that [stand as] the superstratum and the substratum."[13]

[2.2] The relation between the ether and a [flying] bird[14]

However, the purpose [of including the expression, "between entities that stand as the superstratum and the substratum," in the definition] is not to exclude the relation between the ether and a [flying] bird, since it (the relation between the ether and a flying bird) is excluded by virtue of the very expression, "entities that fix without being separate [from each other]."[15]

[3] A cause of the idea "[this is] here" (*ihapratyayahetu*)[16]

Even so, the relation of the denoted and the denoter (*vācyavācakabhāva*) between the ether and the [articulated] word "ether"[17] would be

---

13. Regarding the argument in this [2.1], see B. Shastri [1993: 122] and Bhattacharya [1994: 19–20].
14. TEXT: *na tv ākāśaśakunisambandhanivṛttyartham* ([1]*ayutasiddhapadenaiva*[1]) *tasya nirvarttitatvāt.*
    VARIANTS: (1) S, *ayutasiddhipadenaiva.*
15. In the chapter of disjunction (*vibhāga*), Śrīdhara admits that separate existence is between the ether and a [flying] bird as follows: "[Praśastapāda says that] 'to the contrary, as to the transient entities, separate existence [means] inhering in separate loci.' [I will comment on it:] as to the transient entities, two [transient entities] or one [of them] inhere in different loci apart from each other. 'Inherering' [in the statement by Praśastapāda means] residing of two entities in different loci. Moreover, as to a [flying] bird and the ether, the other entity, the [flying] bird, resides in a locus other than [the ether]." (The *NK*, p. 160,10–13: *anityānāṃ tu yuteṣv āśrayeṣu samavāyo yutasiddhiḥ. dvayor anyatarasya vā parasparaparihāreṇānyatrāśraye samavāyo yutasiddhir anityānāṃ. dvayoḥ pṛthagāśrayāśrayitvaṃ* ([1]*samavāyaḥ*[1]). *śakunyākāśayoś cānyatarasya śakuneḥ pṛthagāśrayāśrayitvam.*) The O edition (p. 384,2) shows variants with regard to (1): *ghaṭapaṭayoḥ*. Then, regarding the relation between the ether and a [flying] bird, the *Vy* argues that it is excluded by the expression, "the superstratum and the substratum." See section [2] "Entities that [stand as] the superstratum and the substratum" in the translation of the *Vy* in Part II.
16. TEXT: *evam apy ākāśasyākāśapadasya ca vācyavācakabhāvaḥ samavāyaḥ syāt. tannivṛttyartham ihapratyayahetur iti. vācyavācakabhāve hi tasmāc chabdāt tadartho jñāyate na tv ihedam iti.*
17. As an example under the relation of the denoted and the denoter, the *Vy* also shows the relation of the ether and the [articulated] word "ether." On this relation, see Figure 4 in Chapter 3. Regarding "the [articulated] word 'ether,'" the *Vy* uses the Sanskrit term "*ākāśaśabda*," whereas the *NK* uses "*ākāśapada*."

inherence. In order to exclude it (the relation of the denoted and the denoter) [from the concept of inherence, Praśastapāda includes the expression] "a cause of the idea '[this is] here.'" The reason [why "a cause of the idea 'this is here'" can exclude the relation of the denoted and the denoter] is that, in the case of the relation of the denoted and denoter, [the idea that] the meaning of its [word] is known from the word [occurs], but [the idea that] "this is here" (the denoter is in the denoted) does not [occur].[18]

[4] Entities that fix without being separate [from each other] (*ayutasiddha*)

[4.1] The relation between a bowl and a fruit of jujube[19]

[When inherence is defined as "the relation], which is a cause of the idea '[this is] here,' between entities that [stand as] the superstratum and the substratum," the relation between a bowl and a fruit of jujube is not excluded [from the concept of inherence]. Therefore, [Praśastapāda places the expression in the definition,] "between entities that fix without being separate [from each other]."[20]

See section [4.2] "The relation of the denoted and the denoter, and that of an object and the cognition of the object—2" in the translation of the *Vy* in Part II.

18. The narrow application (*avyāpti*) of the definition of inherence is pointed out in this case. That is to say, although the Vaiśeṣika doctrine admits that the relation between the ether and the articulated word "ether" is inherence, the relation is excluded from the concept of inherence by the expression "a cause of the idea '[this is] here'." However, even though the definition has the defect of narrow application, it is regarded as a correct definition in Indian philosophy. On this point, see Matilal [1990 (1985): 176–202] and Sato [1995: 25–27]. Moreover, regarding the argument in [3], see B. Shastri [1993: 123] and Bhattacharya [1994: 21–22].
19. TEXT: *ādhāryādhārabhūtānām ihapratyayahetur iti kuṇḍabadarasambandho na vyavacchidyate tadartham ayutasiddhānām iti.*
20. The relation between a bowl and a fruit of jujube subsists between entities that stand as the superstratum (the fruit of jujube) and the substratum (the bowl), and causes the idea, "the fruit of jujube is in the bowl." However, this relation does not subsist between entities that fix without being separate from each other, since the bowl and the fruit of jujube are entities that fix separately (*yutasiddha*). On this relation, see Figure 1 in Chapter 3.

[4.2] Objection to the expression *ayutasiddha*[21]

On this point, some people[22] state a dilemma on the word of "*ayutasiddha*," [that is to say, does the word mean that] two separate entities do *not* exist, or that two *inseparate* entities exist?[23] If [it means that] two separate entities do *not* exist, what is the relation between the two entities? [In this case, there is not any relation between them] since two possessors (relata) of property (relation) do not exist.[24] If [it means that] two *inseparate* entities exist, even so, what ever would be the relation [between the two entities]? [There is not any relation between them] since [the two entities] exist as being non-different entities at all. Indeed, a relation is between two distinct entities, for instance, between a bowl and a fruit of jujube.[25]

---

21. TEXT: *atra kecid* [(1)]*ayutasiddhapadaṃ*[(1)] *vikalpayanti kiṃ yutau na siddhau āhosvid ayutau siddhau. yadi yutau na siddhau kas tayoḥ sambandho dharmiṇor abhāvāt. athāyutau siddhau tathāpi kaḥ sambandho 'pṛthaksiddhatvād eva. bhinnayor hi sambandho yathā kuṇḍabadarayor iti.*
VARIANTS: (1) R, S, *ayutasiddhipadaṃ*.
22. According to the *Nyāyakusumodgama* (p. 50,18), which is a commentary on the *NK*, "some people" (*kecid*) indicates the propounder of identity relation (*tādātmya*), who does not tolerate inherence relation. (*na hi bhavati rūpe rasa iti samavāyam asahamānāṃs tādātmyavādina utthāpayanti atra kecid iti.*)
23. The different point of two alternative views for the word "*ayutasiddha*" is that which the negative participle "*a*" modifies—*siddha* or *yuta*. In the former case, "*ayutasiddha*" means that two entities do *not* exist as being separate. In the later case, it means that two entities exist as being *inseparate*.
24. In this case, property (*dharma*) stands for a relation and property-possessors (*dharmin*) stand for the relata (two entities).
25. On the argument in [4.2], see B. Shasrtri [1993: 123].

[4.3] Answer to the objection[26]

Others[27] do not accept it (the statement of dilemma on the word of "*ayutasiddha*" mentioned above). Indeed this (the word of "*ayutasiddha*") does not have such a meaning [as "two separate entities do not exist."] The reason [for this] is that "two separate entities do not exist" [means that two separate entities] do not arise, so that inherence is not recognized between non-beings. Moreover, this (the word of "*ayutasiddha*") does not have such a meaning [as "two inseparate entities exist"] since "two inseparate entities exist" [means that] two entities exist with identity. Indeed, if [two entities] are identical, there will be a single entity, not two entities, since the property of possessing a nature of two entities has a character of absence of identity. And [in the case of inherence, both relata] are not in reality an identical entity.[28] The reasons [for this] are that both forms of the two [entities] appear as distinct from each other,[29] [and that] the very

---

26. TEXT: *tadapare na* [(1]*mṛṣyanti*[1)]. *na hy* [(2]*asyāyam artho*[2)]. *yutau na siddhau na niṣpannāv iti asatoḥ samavāyānabhyupagamāt. nāpy asyāyam arthaḥ. ayutau siddhāv* [(3]*ekātmakau siddhāv*[3)] *iti ekātmakatve hy ekam eva vastu syān nobhayam. parasparātmakatvābhāvalakṣaṇatvād ubhayarūpatāyāḥ. na ca tadekaṃ vastu paramārthataḥ. parasparavilakṣaṇena rūpeṇa tayor ākārayoḥ pratibhāsanāt. vilakṣaṇākārabuddhivedyatvasyaiva bhedalakṣaṇatvāt. anyathā bhedābhedavyavasthānupapatteḥ. tasmān na svarūpābhedo 'py ayutasiddhiḥ kiṃ tv ayutasiddhānām iti parasparaparihāreṇa pṛthagāśrayānāśritānām ity arthaḥ. tathā ca sati sambandho nānupapannaḥ. svarūpabhedasya sambhavād bhinnayoś ca parasparopaśleṣasya dahanāyaḥpiṇḍayor iva vinā sambandhenāsambhavāt.*
VARIANTS: (1) R, S, *mṛṣanti*; (2) S, *ayam asyārtho*; (3) R, S omit.
27. The *Pañjikā* (p. 50,16–17), which is a commentary on the *NK*, interprets "*apare* (others)" as the Vaiśeṣikas (*apare vaiśeṣikāḥ*).
28. According to the *Pañjikā* (p. 51,16), the word "*tad*" in "*na ca tadekaṃ vastu*" signifies nature (*svarūpa*) of two entities, for instance, the threads and the cloth (*tad iti tantupaṭasvarūpam*).
29. On this portion, the *Nyāyakusumodgama* (p. 50,23–24) comments that "the cloth is in the threads" [and] "cowness is in the cows," since both entities that fix without being separate [from each other], [for instance,] the parts and the whole [and] the universal and the possessor of universal, appear as possessing the properties of number and so on which are inconsistent with the other, it is unsuitable that [both entities] are identical. (*parasparavilakṣaṇeneti iha tantuṣu paṭaḥ iha goṣu gotvam ityevam ayutasiddhayor avayavāvayavinor jātijātimatoḥ parasparaviruddhasaṅkhyādidharmavattayā pratibhāsanād ekatvam ayuktam, ...*)

property of being known by cognition of distinct forms is the character of difference. Otherwise, it would be impossible to separate between difference (*bheda*) and identity (*abheda*). Therefore, "*ayutasiddhi*" does not [mean] identity (*svarūpābheda*) [of two entities] either, but [the word of] "*ayutasiddhānām*" means "between entities that do not reside in different loci apart from each other." And this being the case, it would not be impossible for a relation to exist [between entities that fix without being separate from each other] since a different nature [in each of two inseparate entities] is possible and a close mutual contact between distinct entities is not possible without a relation, like that between fire and an iron ball.[30]

[4.4] Difference between inherence and conjunction[31]

However, the only difference [between conjunction and inherence] is as follows:[32] [In the case of conjunction,] after fire occurs, [fire]

---

30. Regarding the compound of *dahanāyaḥpiṇḍayor*, Honda [1990: 27] translates it into "between the two firing iron balls, not "between fire and an iron ball." Although conjunction is found in each case, I translate it into "between fire and an iron ball" as Jhā [1982 (1915): 34] does. In addition, see the following translation in [4.4] which argues for the relationship between fire and an iron ball not between the two firing iron balls. Regarding the argument in [4.3], see B. Shastri [1993: 123–124].

31. TEXT: *iyāṃs tu viśeṣo, vahnir utpatteḥ paścād ayaḥpiṇḍena saha sambaddhyate, iha tu svakāraṇasāmarthyād upajāyamānam eva tatra sambaddhyate, yathā chidikriyā chedyenety alam.*

32. Jhā [1982 (1915): 34] translates this portion into "The only difference however between ordinary relationship and Inherence is this: [...]." He does not explain what "ordinary relationship" indicates. Following Honda [1990: 27] and the commentaries on the *NK*, I understand that this portion mentions the only difference between "conjunction" and inherence. The *Nyāyakusumodgama* (p. 51,25–26) comments that "[the phrase of] 'however, the only [difference]' means that there is non-connection, which has a state of having not connected formerly, between both the threads and the cloth, like fire and an iron ball." (*iyāṃs tv iti. na tantupaṭayor dahanāyaḥpiṇḍavad aprāptir pūrvikā prāptir ity arthaḥ.*) This comment brings the definition of conjunction in the *PDhS* to mind. On the definition of conjunction, the *NK* (p. 146,8–10) comments as follows: "[The *PDhS* defines that] 'conjunction is connection of two entities that were not connected'. [I will comment on it:] that which is the connection [or] the close contact with each other of two substances that were not connected formerly is conjunction. [The expression of 'two entities] that were not connected' aims to distinguish [conjunction] from inherence." (*aprāptayoḥ prāptiḥ saṃyogaḥ. pūrvam aprāptayor dravyayoḥ paścād yo prāptiḥ parasparasaṃśleṣaḥ sa saṃyogaḥ aprāptayor iti samavāyavyavacchedārtham.*)

has a relation to an iron ball.[33] On the other hand, in this case of [inherence], being born by the power of its own causes, it (the effect or the product)[34] is simultaneously related to it (the cause).[35] For instance, the action of cutting off [is simultaneously related to] what is to be cut off.[36] [We have done] enough of [this consideration of inherence].

33. See fn. 30 in this Part III.
34. For instance, cloth is applicable for the effect or the product. See the *Pañjikā*, p. 51,18: *upajāyamānam eveti paṭādi*.
35. For instance, the threads are applicable for the cause. See the *Pañjikā*, p. 51,18: *tatreit tantvādau*. On the "theory of simultaneity" and the "dilemma about being and non-being" in reference to the term *sāmārthya*, see Halbfass [1993 (1992): 194–196].
36. Regarding this instance, B. Shastri [1993: 121–122] explains as follows: "the act of felling (*chidi kriyā*) emerges simultaneously with its relations with the tree."

PART IV

AN ANNOTATED TRANSLATION OF THE DEFINITION OF INHERENCE (*SAMAVĀYA*) CHAPTER IN THE *KIRAṆĀVALĪ*

In Part IV I provide an annotated translation of the "definition of inherence" chapter in the *Kiraṇāvalī* (*Kir*) of Udayana (ca. 1050–1100). The *Kir* is a commentary on the *PDhS*, together with the *Vy*, the *NK* etc. We have the following printed texts of the *Kir*:

A: *Kiraṇāvalī by Udayanācāryya with the Commentary of Vardhamānopādhyāya, Fasc. I–III*, edited by M.M. Siva Chandra Sārvvabhouma, Bibliotheca Indica: A Collection of Oriental Works, Reprint, Calcutta: The Asiatic Society, 1989.

B: *The Aphorisms of the Vaiśeshika Philosophy by Kaṇāda with the Commentary of Praśastapāda, and the Gloss of Udayanācārya*, edited by Vindhyeśvarī Prasāda Dvivedī, Benares Sanskrit Series, Nos. 15, 50, 155, 156, and 157, Benares: Braj Bhushan Das & Co., 1919.

G: *Kiraṇāvalī by Udayanācārya*, edited and translated by Gaurīnātha Śāstrī, Gaṅgānāthajhā Granthamālā vol. 8, Varanasi: Research Institute, Sampurnanand Sanskrit Vishvavidyalaya, 1980.

O: *Praśastapādabhāṣyam with the Commentary Kiraṇāvalī of Udayanācārya*, edited by J.S. Jetly, Gaekwad's Oriental Series 154, Vadodara: Oriental Institute, Reprint, 1991.

S: *Kiraṇāvalīrahasyam of M.M. Mathurānātha Tarkavāgīśa*, edited by Gaurīnātha Śāstrī, M.M. Śivakumāraśāstrī Granthamālā vol. 4, Varanasi: Sampurnanand Sanskrit Vishvavidyalaya, 1981.

In this Part, I have edited Udayana's text, using the above five editions. Of these five, I have used mainly the O edition. The passages from the other editions are given as variants in the footnotes. When a passage of another edition is used, the passage of the O edition is given as a variant. Based on the edited Udayana text, I make a translation of the "definition of inherence" chapter in the *Kir*. In translating it, I have also consulted three commentaries on the *Kir*: the *Kiraṇāvalīṭīkā* of Bhaṭṭa Vādīndra (ca. 1225), the *Kiraṇāvalīprakāśa* of Vardhamāna (fl. 1350–1375), and the *Kiraṇāvalīrahasya* of Mathurānātha Tarkavāgīśa (fl. 1550–1590).[1] The synopsis of the chapter of inherence's definition in the *Kir* is supplied for convenient reference. This synopsis was

1. Regarding the commentaries on the *Kir* and the dating of the three commentators, see Thakur [2003: 295–298].

made by myself, in consideration of the contents of the *Kir*, elucidating information that is often implied but not explicitly shown in the Sanskrit text itself. In the translation, words enclosed by square brackets are words which I have supplied. And words enclosed by round brackets are added to clarify the meaning or significance of ambiguous words in the English translation, or are the original Sanskrit words.

Regarding translations, while no scholar has yet completely translated the chapter of inherence's definition in the *Kir* into English, B.K. Matilal has offered a summary in Potter (ed.) [1995b (1977): 590]. Honda [2009b] has provided a Japanese translation of the whole *Kir*.

The Synopsis of the Chapter of Inherence's Definition in the *Kiraṇāvalī*

[1] Entities that fix without being separate [from each other] (*ayutasiddha*)

[1.1] Consideration of *ayutasiddha*

[1.2] The relation of conjunction (*saṃyoga*)

[2] Entities that [stand as] the superstratum and the substratum (*ādhāryādhārabhūta*)

[3] A cause of the idea "[this is] here" (*ihapratyayahetu*)

A Translation of the Chapter of Inherence's Definition in the *Kiraṇāvalī*

[1] Entities that fix without being separate [from each other] (*ayutasiddha*)

[1.1] Consideration of *ayutasiddha*[2]

Since inherence is single, there is no division [among inherence]. Therefore, [Praśastapāda] describes the definition [of inherence, without mentioning its division, as] "between entities that fix without being separate [from each other] (*ayutasiddha*)." Since these [entities] are not only separate (*ayuta*) [or] connected (*prāpta*), but also fixed (*siddha*), [the word] "*ayutasiddhāḥ*" means [that those entities which] are only connected with [and] are not separate [from each other]. The relation between them is inherence, which is of a character of connection (*prāpti*).[3]

2. TEXT: *samavāyasyaikatvād vibhāgo* (1*nāstīti*1) *lakṣaṇam āha ayutasiddhānām iti. ayutāḥ prāptāś ca* (2*te siddhāś cety*2) *ayutasiddhāḥ prāptā eva santi* (3*na viyuktā*3) *iti yāvat. teṣāṃ sambandhaḥ prāptilakṣaṇaḥ samavāyaḥ.*
   VARIANTS: (1) S, *na sambhavatīti*; (2) A, G, S, *siddhā iti*; (3) A, G, *nāprāptā*.
3. Connection (*prāpti*) means direct relation; that is to say, where there is nothing in between two relata. On the concept of connection, to quote B. Shastri [1993: 146, n. 51], "Relation means getting into contact, and this implies direct relation. In other words, the two relata of which are not intervened by any other entities except the relation that is the direct relation. Both *saṁyoga* and *samavāya* are direct relations, because nothing intervenes between the relata of the above two relations. In contrast to this the relation between the son and the farther may be cited. The two are related by the relation of *janya-janaka-bhava* [*bhāva*] (the son is off-spring and the farther is progenitor) but their relation is not the direct relation—time and space intervening between the two."

[1.2] The relation of conjunction (*saṃyoga*)[4]

The relation of conjunction is excluded by virtue of it (the word, "*ayutasiddha*"),[5] since it (the relation of conjunction) is preceded by non-connection (*aprāpti*).[6] Accordingly, the definition that "inherence is eternal connection" is very suitable. [Praśastapāda] will state that there is no eternal conjunction.[7] On the other hand, inherence is eternal.[8]

---

4. TEXT: *tena* (1*saṃyogasambandho*1) *vyavacchinnaḥ,* (2*tasyāprāptipūrvakatvāt*2). *tathā ca* (3*nityā prāptiḥ*3) *samavāya iti lakṣaṇaṃ sūcitaṃ* (4*bhavati*4). *ajasaṃyogābhāvo vakṣyate, samavāyasya nityatvaṃ ca.*
VARIANTS: (1) A, *sambandho*; B, O, G, *saṃyogo*; (2) A, *tasyāprāptipravarttakatvāt*; (3) A, G, S, *nityaprāptiḥ*; (4) A, G, S omit.
5. The *Kiraṇāvalīrahasya* (p. 88,8–9) comments that *tena* indicates *siddha* in the word of *ayutasiddha* (*siddhaviśeṣaṇaprayojanam āha teneti. arthataḥ siddhaviśeṣanopādānenety arthaḥ*).
6. The *PDhS* (no. 168) defines conjunction as follows: "conjunction is connection of two entities that were not connected (*aprāptayoḥ prāptiḥ saṃyogaḥ*)." The *Kir* comments on this definition as follows: "connection (*prāpti*) means touching. And since inherence is also it (connection), [the words] "of two entities that were not connected" is mentioned [in the *PDhS*]. However, inherence does not exist between two entities that were not connected, since the moment [one entity] emerges it is related to [the other entity]. A contact of two entities that exist and were not connected is conjunction, whereas inherence is not so. Therefore, it (inherence) is excluded." (*Kir* (O), 145,3–6: *prāptiḥ saṃśleṣaḥ. sa ca samavāyo 'pīty ato uktam aprāptayor iti. samavāyas tv aprāptayor na bhavaty eva, jātaḥ saṃbaddhaś cety ekakālatvāt vidyamānayor aprāptayoḥ saṃśleṣaḥ saṃyogaḥ. samavāyas tu naivam ity asya vyavacchedaḥ*). Moreover, the *PDhS* (no. 183) defines disjunction (*vibhāga*) as follows: "disjunction is non-connection which is preceded by connection [among two entities]" (*prāptipūrvikā 'prāptir vibhāgaḥ*).
7. In the chapter of conjunction in the *PDhS* (no. 166–178), Praśastapāda denies unborn and eternal conjunction, referring to the three kinds of conjunctions: *sa ca trividhaḥ. anyatarakarmajaḥ ubhayakarmajaḥ saṃyogajaś ca. ... nāsty ajaḥ saṃyogo nityaparimaṇḍalavat pṛthag anabhidhānāt.* Regarding Udayana's commentary on this portion, see the *Kir* (p. 148,11–14).
8. Udayana admits that both inherence and conjunction are connection, but does not admit that conjunction is eternal. Therefore, adding the word "eternal" to connection, conjunction can be distinguished from inherence. According to the statement in [1.1] in this chapter, we may say that the entities between which conjunction subsists are in the condition of inseparate or connected, but are not in the condition of fixed or firm since these entities are not constantly in the condition of inseparate or connected.

[2] Entities that [stand as] the superstratum and the substratum (*ādhāryādhārabhūta*)[9]

[Inclusion of] the relation, which is characterized by the state of the denoted and the denoter etc., [in the concept of inherence] would not result by virtue of the very word of "connection" (*prāpti*).[10] In order to make this clear, [Praśastapāda says,] "between entities that [stand as] the superstratum and the substratum." In other words, [the relation] of the superstratum and the substratum [occurs] naturally and not by accidental attribute.[11]

---

9. TEXT: *prāptipadenaiva* (1*vācyavācakādibhāvalakṣaṇaḥ*1) (2*sambandho*2) *na prasajyate. etadeva spaṣṭayati ādhāryādhārabhūtānām iti.* (3*svabhāvād*3) (4*ādhāryādhārāṇāṃ*4) *na tv āgantukena dharmeṇety arthaḥ.*
   VARIANTS: (1) B, O, *vācyavācakabhāvādilakṣaṇaḥ*; G, *vācyavācakādibhāva-lakṣaṇasambandho*; (2) G omits; (3) B, O, *svabhāvata*; (4) A, G, S, *ādhāryādhāraṇaṃ*.
10. Udayana defines inherence as "eternal connection." The word, "eternal," cannot exclude the relation of the denoted and the denoter from the concept of inherence, since it is also eternal. The reason for its eternality is that the relation of the denoted and the denoter is dependent on the desire of God, which itself is eternal. See the *Kiraṇāvalīprakāśa* (p. 134,5–6): *prāptipadeneti. na ca nityapadeṇaiva tannirāsaḥ. asyeśvarecchārūpatayā nityatvāt.* Therefore, Udayana insists that the relation should be excluded by the word, "connection." Regarding this, see B. Shastri [1993: 129]. Moreover, as we pointed out regarding the concept of connection (*prāpti*) in fns. 3 and 6, this includes conjunction and inherence but excludes another relation that is self-linking relation (*svarūpasambandha*). The denoted and the denoter are included in self-linking relation, so that this is not applied to the definition of inherence by virtue of the word, connection. Regarding the difference between self-linking relation and conjunction/inherence, Jha [1990: xxv–xxix] explains this based on the Navya-nyāya doctrine.
11. We can see Udayana's thought that the relation of the denoted and the denoter is established by accidental attribute. According to the Nyāya-Vaiśeṣika, the relation of the denoted and the denoter is not natural, but conventional. That is to say, the relation occurs not naturally, but through the accidental attribute of the convention (*saṃketa*) via the will of God. On this point see K. Kunjunni Raja [2000 (1963): 19–25] and Ḍhuṇḍhirāja's interpretation of the definition of inherence in the *Padārthadharmasaṃgraha* (C) (p. 5). On the contrary, since the relation of the superstratum and the substratum occurs naturally, it can exclude the relation of the denoted and the denoter from the concept of inherence.

[3] A cause of the idea "[this is] here" (*ihapratyayahetu*)[12]

In this [definition, Praśastapāda] describes a means of getting valid cognition (*pramāṇa*): a cause of the idea "[this is] here (this is in that)." It means that such ideas as "cloth is in the threads," "whiteness is in the cloth," "cowness is in the cow," and so forth, which do not occur by virtue of something other than relation, prove [the real existence of] it (inherence).[13]

---

12. TEXT: ([1]*tatra*[1]) *pramāṇam āha ihapratyayahetur iti. iha tantuṣu* ([2]*paṭa*[2]) *iha paṭe śuklatvam iha gavi gotvam ityādayaḥ* ([3]*pratyayāḥ*[3]) *sambandham* ([4]*antareṇānupapadyamānās*[4]) *taṃ vyavasthāpayantīty arthaḥ.*
VARIANTS: (1) B, O omit; (2) G, *paṭaḥ*; (3) A omits; (4) S, *antareṇānupapannās.*
13. On the relationship of an object and its cognition in Vaiśeṣika philosophy, see 1.3 "The Concept of Inherence" in Chapter 1.

BIBLIOGRAPHY AND ABBREVIATIONS

PRIMARY SOURCES

Aṣṭādhyāyī (*Pāṇinisūtra*) of Pāṇini, see *Pāṇiniśūtra*.

Kir: *Kiraṇāvalī* (O).

Kiraṇāvalī (B) of Udayana, in *The Aphorisms of the Vaiśeshika Philosophy by Kaṇāda with the Commentary of Praśastapāda, and the Gloss of Udayanācārya*, edited by Vindhyeśvarī Prasāda Dvivedī, Benares Sanskrit Series, Nos. 15, 50, 155, 156, and 157, Benares: Braj Bhushan Das & Co., 1919.

Kiraṇāvalī (G) of Udayana, in *Kiraṇāvalī by Udayanācārya*, edited and translated by Gaurīnātha Śāstrī, Gaṅgānāthajhā Granthamālā vol. 8, Varanasi: Research Institute, Sampurnanand Sanskrit Vishvavidyalaya, 1980.

Kiraṇāvalī (BI) of Udayana, in *Kiraṇāvalī by Udayanācāryya*, edited by Narendra Chandra Vedantatirtha, Bibliotheca Indica: A Collection of Oriental Works, Calcutta: The Asiatic Society, 1956.

Kiraṇāvalī (A) of Udayana, in *Kiraṇāvalī by Udayanācāryya with the Commentary of Vardhamānopādhyāya, Fasc. I–III*, edited by M.M. Siva Chandra Sārvvabhouma, Bibliotheca Indica: A Collection of Oriental Works, Reprint, Calcutta: The Asiatic Society, 1989.

Kiraṇāvalī (S) of Udayana, in *Kiraṇāvalīrahasyam of M.M. Mathurānātha Tarkavāgīśa*, edited by Gaurīnātha Śāstrī, M.M. Śivakumāraśāstrī Granthamālā vol. 4, Varanasi: Sampurnanand Sanskrit Vishvavidyalaya, 1981.

Kiraṇāvalī (O) of Udayana, in *Praśastapādabhāṣyam with the Commentary Kiraṇāvalī of Udayanācārya*, edited by J.S. Jetly, Gaekwad's Oriental Series 154, Vadodara: Oriental Institute, Reprint, 1991.

Kiraṇāvalīprakāśa of Vardhamāna, see *Kiraṇāvalī* (A).

Kiraṇāvalīrahasya of Mathurānātha Tarkavāgīśa, see *Kiraṇāvalī* (S).

Kiraṇāvalīṭīkā of Bhaṭṭa Vādīndra, see *Kiraṇāvalī* (BI).

Lakṣaṇāvalī of Udayana, in Tachikawa [1981].

Mahābhāṣya of Patañjali, in *The Vyākaraṇa-mahābhāṣya of Patañjali*; 3 Vols., edited by K.V. Abhyankar, Poona: Bhandarkar Oriental Research Institute.

Manusmṛti, in Manusmṛti with nine Commentaries by Medhātithi, Sarvajñanārāyaṇa, Kullūka, Raghavānanda, Nandana, Rāmacandra, Maṇirāma, Govindarāja and Bhāruci, 6 Vols., edited by Jayantakrishna Harikrishna Dave, Bhāratīya Vidyā Series 29, 33, 37, 38–40, Bombay: Bharatiya Vidya Bhavan, 1972–84.

NK: *Nyāyakandalī* (S).

Nyāyabhāṣya of Vātsyāyana, in *Nyāyadarśanam*, edited with Vātsyāyana's *Bhāṣya*, Uddyotakara's *Vārttika*, Vācaspati Miśra's *Tātparyaṭīkā*, and Viśvanātha's *Vṛtti* by Taranatha Nyaya-Tarkatirtha and Amarendramohan Tarkatirtha, Calcutta: Munishiram Manoharlal Publishers, 1985.

Nyāyabhūṣaṇa of Bhāsarvajña, in *ŚrīmadācāryabhāsarvajñapraṇītasyaNyāyas ārasya Svopajñaṃ Vyākyānāṃ Nyāyabhūṣaṇam*, edited by Svāmī Yogīndrānanda, Ṣaḍdarśanaprakāśanagranthamālā 1, Vārāṇasī: Ṣaḍdarśana Prakāśana Pratiṣṭhānam, 1968.

Nyāyakandalī (O) of Śrīdhara, in *Nyāyakandalī being a Commentary on Praśastapādabhāṣya, with Three Sub-commentaries*, edited by J.S. Jetly and Vasant G. Parikh, Gaekwad's Oriental Series 174, Vadodara: Oriental Institute, 1991.

Nyāyakandalī (S) of Śrīdhara, in *the Praśastapāda Bhāshya with Commentary Nyāyakandalī of Śrīdhara*, edited by Vindhyesvari Prasad Dvivedin, Sri Garib Dass Oriental Series 13, Delhi: Sri Satguru Publications, 1984.

Nyāyakandalī (R) of Śrīdhara, in *Praśastapādabhāṣya (Padārthadharmasaṃgraha) with Commentary Nyāyakandalī by Śrīdhara Bhatta*, edited with Hindi Translation by Durgādhara Jhā, Gaṅgānātha Jhā Granthamālā vol. 1, Varanasi: Research Institute, Sampurnanand Sanskrit Vishvavidyalaya, 1977.

Nyāyakusumodgama of Śiḍila Vommideva, see *Nyāyakandalī* (O).

Padārthadharmasaṃgraha (C) of Praśastapāda, in *Vaiśeṣikadarśane Maharṣipravara-Praśastadevācārya-viracitaṃ Praśastapāda-bhāṣyaṃ. Vidvaccūḍāmaṇi Śrī Śankaramiśravinirmitaḥ Upaskāraś ca.* Ubhayatra Kāśīsthavedavidyālayādhyāpaka-Nyāyopādhyāya Paṃ. Ḍhuṇḍhirājaśāstri-kṛtaṃ Vivaraṇam, Haridāsasaṃskṛtagranth amālāsamākhya-Kāśīsaṃskṛtasīrijatṛtīyapustakamālāyāḥ 3, Kashi: Chaukhambha, 1923.

Padārthadharmasaṃgraha (*PDhS*) of Praśastapāda, in Bronkhorst and Ramseier [1994].

Pāṇiniśūtra of Pāṇini, in *The Aṣṭādhyāyī of Pāṇini*, edited and translated into English By Śrīśa Chandra Vasu, 2 Vols., Delhi/Varanasi/Patna/Bhangalore/Madras/Calcutta/Mumbai/Pune: Motilal Banrasidass, 1997.

Prameyakamalamārtaṇḍa of Prabhācandra, in *Prameyakamala-Martanḍa* by Shri Prabha Chandra, edited with A Commentary on Shri Manik Nandi's *Pareeksha Mukh Sūtra* and Introduction, Indexes etc. by Mahendra Kumar Shastri, Sri Garib Dass Oriental Series 94, 3rd ed., Delhi: Sri Satguru Publications, 1990.

Pañjikā of Rājaśekhara Sūri, see *Nyāyakandalī* (O).

Ṭippaṇa of Naracandrasūri, see *Nyāyakandalī* (O).

Vaiśeṣikasūtra (*VS*) of Kaṇāda, in *Vaśeṣikasūtra of Kaṇāda*, edited with the commentary of Candrānanda by Jambuvijaya, Gaekwad's Oriental Series 136, 2nd ed., Baroda: Oriental Institute, 1982.

Vaiśeṣikasūtravṛtti of Candrānanda. See *Vaiśeṣikasūtra*.

VS: *Vaiśeṣikasūtra*.

Vy: *Vyomavatī* (S).

Vyomavatī (C) of Vyomaśiva, in *Praśastapādabhāṣyam*, edited with commentaries (up to Dravya) *Sūktī* of Jagadīśa Tarkālaṃkāra, *Setu* of Padmanābha Miśra and *Vyomavatī* of Vyomaśivāchārya (to the end) by M.M. Gopīnath Kavirāj and Panditraj Dhundhirāj Shāstri, Chowkhamba Sanskrit Series 61, Varanasi: Chaukamba Amarabharati Prakashan, 1983.

Vyomavatī (Mys) of Vyomaśiva, *Manuscript of Vyomavatī* belonging to the University of Mysore Oriental Research Institute, Ms.-No. C-1575.

Vyomavatī (S) of Vyomaśiva, in *Vyomavatī of Vyomaśivācārya*, edited with the *Praśastapādabhāṣya* by Gaurinath Sastri, 2 Vols., M.M. Śivakumāraśāstri-granthamālā 6, Varanasi: Sampurnanand Sanskrit University, 1983, 1984.

SECONDARY LITERATURE

Altekar, A.S.

1951 *Education in Ancient India*, 4th ed., Banaras: Nand Kishore and Bros.

Baldick, C.

2001 (1990) *Concise Dictionary of Literary Terms*, 2nd ed., New York: Oxford University Press.

Bhaduri, Sadananda

1975 (1947) *Studies in Nyāya-Vaiśeṣika Metaphisics*, Poona: Bhandarkar Oriental Research Institute.

Bhattacharya, Tushar, Kanti

1994 *Samavāya and the Nyāya-Vaiśeṣika Realism*, Calcutta: Sanskrit Pustak Bhandar.

Bronkhorst, Johannes

2010 "The Context of Indian Philosophy," in T. Wada (ed.), *Indian Philosophy and Text Science*, Delhi: Motilal Banarsidass Publishers Private Limited, pp. 9–30.

Bronkhorst, Johannes and Yves Ramseier

1994 *Word Index to the Praśastapādabhāṣya: a complete word index to the printed editions of the Praśastapādabhāṣya*, Delhi: Motilal Banarsidass, 1994.

Bühler, G.

1886 *The Law of Manu, Translated with Extracts from Seven Commentaries*, The Sacred Books of the East, Vol. 25. Oxford: The Clarendon Press.

Chatterjee, S. and Datta, D.

1984 (1934) *An Introduction to Indian Philosophy*, Reprint, Calcutta: Calcutta University Press.

Chaube, S.P. and Chaube, A.

1999 *Education in Ancient and Medieval India*, New Delhi: Vikas Publishing House PVT Ltd.

Coward, H.G. (ed.)

1996 (1983) *Studies in Indian Thought*, Reprint, Delhi: Motilal Banarsidass.

Dasgupta, S.

1997 (1922) *A History of Indian Philosophy, vol. I*, Reprint, Delhi: Motilal Banarsidass.

Faddegon, B.

1969 (1918) *The Vaiśeṣika-System, Described with the Help of the Oldest Texts*, Amsterdam: Verhandelingen der Koninklijke Akademie van Wetenschappen te Amsterdam. Afdeeling Letterkunde, Nieuwe Reeks, deel 18, no. 2.

Fillizat, Pierre-Sylvain

1975 "La Grammaire Sanskrite de Pāṇini," *La Traversée des Signes*, Paris: Éditions du Seuil, pp. 171–193.

Halbfass, Wilhelm

1993 (1992) *On Being and What There Is*, Sri Garib Dass Oriental Series 168, 1st Indian ed., Delhi: Sri Satguru Publications.

Hirano, Katsunori

2003 "On the System of the Commentary Text in Indian Philosophy," *SITES: Journal of Studies for the Integrated Text Science*, Vol. 1,

No. 1, pp. 81–92.

2004a "Information Transmission System of the Commentary Texts in Indian Philosophy: A New Light Based on Communication Theory," *Tokai-Bukkyo: Journal of Tokai Association of Indian and Buddhist Studies*, No. 49, pp. 21–36. (in Japanese)

2004b "The Two Types of Cognitive Process in the Vaiśeṣika Philosophy," in S. Hino and T. Wada (eds.), *Three Mountains and Seven Rivers: Prof. Musashi Tachikawa's Felicitation Volume*, Delhi: Motilal Banarsidass, pp. 421–429.

2004c "Originality and Quotation: A Study of a Commentary Text's Genesis in Vaiśeṣika Philosophy," *SITES: Journal of Studies for the Integrated Text Science*, Vol. 2, No. 1, pp. 59–74.

2005 "The Interaction between Text and Context: An Aspect of an Indian Philosophic Commentary Text," *SITES: Journal of Studies for the Integrated Text Science*, Vol. 3, No. 1, pp. 45–56.

2006a "The Genesis of Commentary Texts in Ancient India: From a Quotation Theory Viewpoint," *Conflict between Tradition and Creativity in Indian Philosophy: Text and Context*, 21st Century COE Program International Conference Series 7, pp. 37–46.

2006b "Analysis of the Genesis of Texts from Three Viewpoints," *SITES: Journal of Studies for the Integrated Text Science*, Vol. 4, No. 1, pp. 33–44.

2009 "A Mode of Commentary Generation in the *Nyāyakandalī*: On the Relationship between the Text and the Meta-text," *HERSETEC: Journal of Hermeneutic Study and Education of Textual Configuration (SITES II)*, Vol. 3. No. 1, pp. 45–54.

2010a "New Light on the Commentary Texts of Ancient India," in T. Wada (ed.), *Indian Philosophy and Text Science*, Delhi: Motilal Banarsidass Publishers Private Limited, pp. 135–156.

2010b "The Definition of Inherence in the *Kiraṇāvalī* as the Meta-text on the *Padārthadharmasaṃgraha*," *HERSETEC: Journal of Hermeneutic Study and Education of Textual Configuration (SITES II)*, Vol. 4. No. 1, pp. 43–49.

forthcoming "An Annotated Translation of the Definition of Inherence (*samavāya*) Chapter in the *Vyomavatī*," in *Professor Vattanky Festschrift Volume*.

Hiriyanna, M.

1957 *Indian Philosophical Studies, I and II*, Mysore: Kavyalaya Publishers.

Honda, Megumu

1990 *Vaishesika Tetsugaku Taikei* (The System of Vaiśeṣika Philosophy),

Tokyo: Kokusyo-kanko-kai. (in Japanese)

2009a *Vaisheshika Tetsugaku, Jyoukan, Kokuu no Gotoku* (Vaiśeṣika Philosophy, I), Kyoto: Heirakuji Shoten. (in Japanese)

2009b *Vaisheshika Tetsugaku, Gekan, Kouki no Tsuranari* (Vaiśeṣika Philosophy, II), Kyoto: Heirakuji Shoten. (in Japanese)

Ikegami, Yoshihiko

1997 (1984) *Kigouron heno Syoutai* (An Invitation to the Semiotics), Reprint, Tokyo: Iwanami Publishers. (in Japanese)

Jakobson, Roman

2003 (1973) *Ippan Gengogaku* (Essais de Lingustique Générale), editorial supervision S. Kawamoto, translated by S. Tamura, K. Murasaki, Y. Nagashima, and N. Nakano, Tokyo: Misuzu Shobo. (in Japanese)

Jhā, Gaṅgāṇātha

1982 (1915) *Padārthadharmasaṅgraha of Praśastapāda, With the Nyāyakandalī of Śrīdhara (English Translation)*, Chaukhambha Oriental Studies 4, Reprint, Varanasi/Delhi: Chaukhambha Orientalia.

Jha, V.N.

1990 *The Philosophy of Relations (Containing the Sanskrit Text and English Translation of Dharmakīrti's Sambandha-parīkṣā with Prabācandra's Commentary)*, Bibliotheca Indo-Buddhica 66, Delhi: Sri Satguru Publications.

Kajiyama, Yuichi

1966 "Bukkyotetugaku niokeru Meidaikaishaku—eva no Bunisei-genkinou—" (The Interpretation of the Proposition in Buddhist Philosophy), *Kanakurahakase Kokikinen Indogaku Bukkyogaku Ronsyu*, Kyoto: Heirakuji Shoten. (in Japanese)

Kanakura, Ensho

1971 *Indo no Shizen Tetsugaku* (Philosophy of Nature in India), Kyoto: Heirakuji Shoten. (in Japanese)

Kane, P.V.

1974 *History of Dharmaśāstra Vol. II*, Part I. 2nd ed., Gaverment Series Class B, No. 6, Poona: Bhandarkar Oriental Research Institute.

Kannu, S. Peeru

1992 *The Critical Study of Praśastapādabhāṣya*, Delhi: Kanishka Publishing House.

Keay, F.E.

1918 *Ancient Indiar Education, An Inquiry into its Origin, Development, and Ideals*, London: Oxford University Press.

Kristeva, J.

1969 *Σημειωτική: Recherches pour une Sémanalyse*, Paris: Éditions du Seuil.

Marui, Hiroshi

2002 "Iwayuru Roppa Tetsugaku to iu Gainen ni tsuite--Senko-kenkyugaikan wo Chuusintoshite" (On the Concept of the so-called Six Systems: A Survey of the Previous Studies), in *Kimura Kiyotaka Hakase Kanreki Kinen Ronsyu, Higashi Ajia Bukkyo--sono Seiritsu to Tenkai* (In Honour of Dr. Kiyotaka Kimura on His Sixtieth Birthday), Tokyo: Shunjusha, pp. 677-690.

Matilal, B.K.

1977 "Nyāya-Vaiśeṣika," *A History of Indian Literature*, Vol. 6, Fasc. 2, edited by Jan Gonda, Wiesbaden: Otto Harrassowitz.

1990 (1985) *Logic, Language and Reality*, 2nd ed., Delhi: Motilal Banarsidass.

Matsuzawa, Kazuhiro

2003 *Seiseiron no Tankyu* (Inquiry into Genesis), Nagoya: Nagoya University Press. (in Japanese)

Mazumder, N.N.

1916 *A History of Education in Ancient India*, Calcutta/Bombay/Madras/London: Macmillan & Co., LTD.

McLuhan, Marshall

1964 *Understanding Media: The Extensions of Man*, New York: McGraw-Hill Book Company.

Mitra, V.

1964 *Education in Ancient India*, New Delhi: Arya Book Depot.

Miyamoto, Keiichi

1996 *The Metaphysics and Epistemology of the Early Vaiśeṣikas, with an Appendix Daśapadārthī of Candramati (A Translation with a Reconstructed Sanskrit Text, Notes and a Critical Edition of the Chinese Version)*, Bhandarkar Oriental Series No. 28, Pune: Bhandarkar Oriental Research Institute.

2008 *Indo no Tagenron Tetsugaku wo Yomu*, Praśastapāda *Padārthadharmasaṃgraha* (A Study of Pluralistic Philosophy in India, Translation of the *Padārthadharmasaṃgraha* of Praśastapāda) Tokyo: Shunjusha. (in Japanese)

Murakami, Shinkan

1997 *Realistic Epistemology of Indian Philosophy: Theories on Perception in the Vaiśeṣika and Naiyātika*, Kyoto: Heirakuji Shoten. (in Japanese)

Nakamura, Hajime

1979 Japanese Translation of the Vaiśeṣika Texts and the *Padārthadharmasaṃgraha*, II. *Padārthadharma-saṃgraha, Annual of the Sanko Research Institute for the Studies of Buddhism, No. 10·11, 1977–8*, 157–316.

Nozawa, Masanobu

1999 "On Vibhāga of the Vaiśeṣika System," *Hokkaido Journal of Indological and Buddhist Studies*, Vol. 14, 112–130.

Patil, Parimal G.

2010 "Consuming Scripture: Philosophical Hermeneutics in Classical India," in T. Wada (ed.), *Indian Philosophy and Text Science*, Delhi: Motilal Banarsidass Publishers Private Limited, pp. 77–99.

Phillips, Stephen H.

1997 (1996) *Classical Indian Metaphysics*, 1st Indian ed., Delhi: Motilal Banarsidass.

Potter, K.H.

1991 *Presuppositions of India's Philosophies*, 1st Indian ed., Delhi: Motilal Banarsidass.

Potter, K.H. (ed.)

1995a (1970) *Encyclopedia of Indian Philosophies, Vol. I: Bibliography*, 3rd Revised ed., Delhi: Motilal Banarsidass.

1995b (1977) *Encyclopedia of Indian Philosophies, Vol. II: Indian Metaphysics and Epistemology: The Tradition of Nyāya-Vaiśeṣika up to Gaṅgeśa*, Reprint, Delhi: Motilal Banarsidass.

Raja, C.K.

1950 *Some Aspect of Education in Ancient India*, The Adyar Library Series No. 73, Madras: The Adyar Library.

Raja, K. Kunjunni

2000 (1963) *Indian Theories of Meaning*, The Adyar Library Series 71, Chennai: The Adyar Library and Research Centre.

Raju, P.T.

1985 *Structural Depths of Indian Thought*, New Delhi: South Asian Publishers.

1992 *The Philosophical Traditions of India*, Delhi: Motilal Banarsidass.

Ramanujam, P.S.

1979 *A Study of Vaiśiṣika Philosophy with Special Reference to Vyomaśivācārya*, Mysore: University of Mysore.

Recanati, Francois

2004 *Literal Meaning*, Cambridge: Cambridge University Press.

Sasaki, Ken-ichi

1990 "Inyou wo Meguru Sansei no Porifoni" (Polyphony of Three Voices on Quotation), in *Translation*, Adventure in Modern Philosophy 5, ed. by H. Ichikawa et al., Tokyo: Iwanami Publisher. (in Japanese)

Sato, Hiroyuki

1995 "Teigi no Teigi" (On the Concept of the Definition in Indian Philosophy), *Bukkyo Bunka* 33 (Academic Series 8), pp. 3–29. (in Japanese)

Scharfe, H.

2002 *Education in Ancient India*, Handbook of Oriental Studies, Section 2 Vol. 16. Leiden/Boston/Köln: Brill.

Sen, Biswanath

1985 *The Concepts of Part and Whole (Avayava and Avayavi)*, Calcutta: Rabindra Bharati University.

Shannon, C.E. and Weaver, W.

1969 *Kominikeshon no Sugakutekiriron* (The Mathematical Theory of Communication), translated by J. Hasegawa and M. Inoue, Tokyo: Meiji Tosho. (in Japanese)

Shastri, Biswanarayan

1993 *Samavāya Foundation of Nyāya-Vaiśeṣika Philosophy*, Delhi: Sharada Publishing House.

Shastri, Dharmendra Nath

1976 (1964) *The Philosophy of Nyāya-Vaiśeṣika and Its Conflict with the Buddhist Dignāga School: Critique of Indian Realism*, Reprint, Delhi/Varanasi: Bharatiya Vidya Prakashan.

Shimoda, Masahiro

2010 "Some Reflections on the History of Buddhist Canons in Ancient India," in T. Wada (ed.), *Indian Philosophy and Text Science*, Delhi: Motilal Banarsidass Publishers Private Limited, pp. 33–57.

Tachikawa, Musashi

1981 *The Structure of the World in Indian Realism*, Studies of Classical India 4, Dordrecht: D. Reidel Publishing Company.

Thakur, Anantalal

2003 *Origin and Development of the Vaiśeṣika System, History of Science, Philosophy and Culture in Indian Civilization, Vol. II. Life, Thought and Culture in India, Part 4*, General Editor D.P. Chattopadhyaya, New Delhi: Centre for Studies in Civilizations.

Tubb, G.A. and Boose, E.R.

2007 *Scholastic Sanskrit, A Manual for Students*, New York: The American Institute of Buddhist Studies at Columbia University.

Ui, H.

1917 *The Vaiśeṣika Philosophy*, Oriental Translation Fund., New Series 24, London: Royal Asiatic Society.

Umesha, Mishra

1987 *Connception on Matter, According to Nyāya-Vaiśeṣika*, Reprint, Delhi: Gian Publishing House.

Uno, Atsushi

1996 *Indo Ronrigaku* (Indian Logic), Kyoto: Hōzōkan. (in Japanese)

Vattanky, John

1984 *Gaṅgeśa's Philosophy of God*, The Adyar Library Series 115, Madras: The Adyar Library and Research Cetre.

Wada, Toshihiro

1990 *Invariable Concomitance in Navya-Nyāya*, Sri Garib Dass Oriental Series 101, Delhi: Sri Satguru Publications.

2007 *The Analytical Method of Navya-Nyāya*, Gonda Indological Studies 14, Groningen: Egbert Forsten.

2010 "The Genesis of Sanskrit Texts and Their Context in Navya-nyāya: From Gaṅgeśa's *Tattvacintāmaṇi* to Its Commentaries," in T. Wada (ed.), *Indian Philosophy and Text Science*, Delhi: Motilal Banarsidass Publishers Private Limited, pp. 183–201.

Watase, Nobuyuki

1991 *Sanskrit Genten Zenyaku, Manu Houten*, (The Law of Manu, The Complete Translation of Sanskrit text), Tokyo: Chūōkōron-sha. (in Japanese)

Whitney, W.D.

1997 (1924) *Sanskrit Grammar*, Delhi: Motilal Banarsidass.

Yamakami, Shodo

1999 *Niyayagakuha no Bukkyo Hihan* (Refutation of the Buddhist Doctrine by the Nyāya school), Kyoto: Heirakuji Shoten. (in Japanese)

INDEX